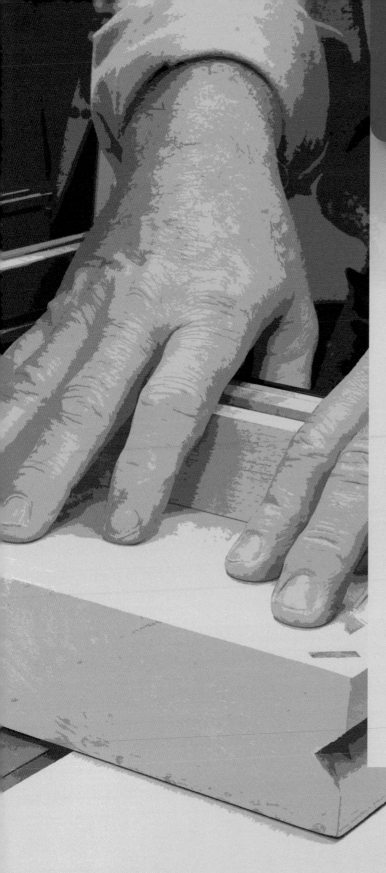

FOREWORD

Down through the ages, woodworkers have crafted boxes for a variety of reasons—both decorative and functional. Of course, the predominant reason is that of storage for anything from documents, photos, collectibles, valuables, and items found in the shop, such as tools and supplies. As either a seasoned or aspiring woodworker, you may like the fact that box making does not typically require a lot of wood. Or you see box making as an opportunity to show off precious pieces of figured wood or your craftsmanship. Still others build boxes as a means to delight loved ones with treasured heirlooms. Whatever your motivation, you'll find that the box designs here will meet all of those needs.

To guarantee your building success, you'll find that each box project contains easy-to-follow step-by-step instructions, dimensioned drawings, how-to photographs, and cut lists. You'll also find lists of suggested products (router bits, hardware, and other supplies) needed to complete the projects.

While some boxes require more care and time in the making, others can be built in a day or two. With each box, you can count on learning new techniques. Lining drawers, working with veneer, and mixing and matching contrasting woods are bonus techniques that will add to your arsenal of skills. And that is to say nothing of the diverse joinery you'll encounter throughout. To help you sort through the selection, the offerings are divided into four categories: Great Gift Boxes, Boxes for the Home, Novelty Boxes, and Boxes for the Shop.

Now, look through the selection, find the box that captures your interest, and start building. Before you are hours of pure woodworking enjoyment, and after that, the beautiful finished project.

SWEETHEART'S MUSIC BOX

By Robert J. Settich and Stephen Johnson

Overall dimensions: 7½"w × 8¼"d × 3½"h

Here's a great gift for Valentine's Day, but you'll find it equally appropriate for a birthday, Mother's Day, a wedding anniversary, or simply as a special surprise. Of course, stocking the two compartments with an additional gift of jewelry will win you extra points.

But even after you give the box away, you'll keep the new skills you developed while making it, among them bandsaw-box making, tricks for cutting and inserting a decorative strip, pattern-routing a shape, flocking, and more.

HOME
WOODWORKER
SERIES

14
WOODEN
BOXES
YOU CAN MAKE

Jim Harrold, EDITOR

Schiffer Publishing Ltd

4880 Lower Valley Road • Atglen, PA 19310

CONTENTS

HOME
WOODWORKER
SERIES

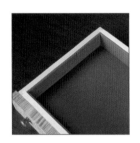

Other Schiffer Books on Related Subjects:

Making Wooden Boxes with Dale Power, 0-7643-0848-3, $14.95

The Fine Art of Marquetry: Creating Images in Wood Using Sawn Veneers, 978-0-7643-3499-3, $39.99

Advance Veneering and Alternative Techniques, 978-0-7643-3846-5, $39.99

Designed by John P. Cheek
Cover by Justin Watkinson

Type set in Helvetica Neue/Calibri/Minion Pro

ISBN: 978-0-7643-4243-1
Printed in China

Published by Schiffer Publishing Ltd.
4880 Lower Valley Road
Atglen, PA 19310
Phone: (610) 593-1777; Fax: (610) 593-2002
E-mail: Info@schifferbooks.com

For the largest selection of fine reference books on this and related subjects, please visit our website at **www.schifferbooks.com**. You may also write for a free catalog.

This book may be purchased from the publisher. Please try your bookstore first.

We are always looking for people to write books on new and related subjects. If you have an idea for a book, please contact us at proposals@schifferbooks.com

Schiffer Books are available at special discounts for bulk purchases for sales promotions or premiums. Special editions, including personalized covers, corporate imprints, and excerpts can be created in large quantities for special needs. For more information contact the publisher.

In Europe, Schiffer books are distributed by
Bushwood Books
6 Marksbury Ave.
Kew Gardens
Surrey TW9 4JF England
Phone: 44 (0) 20 8392 8585; Fax: 44 (0) 20 8392 9876
E-mail: info@bushwoodbooks.co.uk
Website: www.bushwoodbooks.co.uk

Begin with the box body

1 PREPARE THE BLANK FOR THE BOX BODY
(A1, A2, A3). Unless you're fortunate enough to have some 2" thick stock on hand, you'll need to laminate several boards—we used three—to obtain this thickness. Begin by jointing and thickness-planing the stock so that it's flat on both sides. Spread the glue evenly—we used Titebond III—following the advice in the **Tip Alert**. Stack the pieces, making sure that the grain direction is parallel in every layer. Clamp securely, and let dry overnight.

> **TIP ALERT**
> Spread glue quickly over a large surface with a disposable applicator such as a business card or playing card. Plastic cards such as digital hotel "keys" or gift cards can endure repeated uses. Simply wipe clean and store near your glue.

2 SET UP YOUR BANDSAW with a sharp blade that's thin enough to negotiate the curves in this project. A ¼" blade with 6 teeth per inch will give you good results. Carefully square your table to the blade, and adjust your blade guides. Hook up your shop vacuum or dust collector to the bandsaw for the reasons explained in the **Tip Alert**.

3 MAKE PHOTOCOPIES OF THE FULL-SIZED
PATTERNS (see pages 12 and 13). You'll need one copy of the box body pattern and two copies of the lid/base pattern. Adhere the box body pattern to the block with spray adhesive. Note that the grain direction indicated on the pattern runs from top to bottom. Use an awl to mark the centerpoints of the hinge mortises and spring-rod hole.

4 BANDSAW
THE BOX BODY,
following the cutting sequence shown on the full-sized pattern and referring to **Photo A**. Note that the first slice is a relief cut that lets the waste fall free at the end of the second cut instead of requiring you to back out the blade. Stop the relief cut about ¹/₁₆" from the

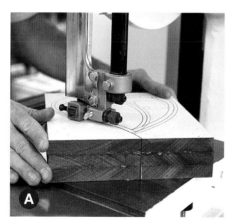

Avoid any sideways pressure on the blade that could produce an out-of-square edge.

outline on the pattern. Make cuts 2 and 3 just to the waste side of the line because you'll sand the edge to the cutline.

Especially on the interior cuts (5 and 6), don't back up if your blade strays slightly from the cutline. Instead, gradually steer the blade back to the cutline.

> **TIP ALERT**
> Some people experience allergic reactions to various hardwoods—especially tropical varieties such as the paduak chosen for this project. Dust on your skin could generate a rash, and inhaled dust could lead to coughing and other problems. Wearing long sleeves and a respirator is prudent and inexpensive insurance.

5 DISCARD THE PLUG FREED BY CUT 4, or save it for another project. Save the smaller plug resulting from cut 6. This piece, called part A3, will become the cover for concealing the music box movement.

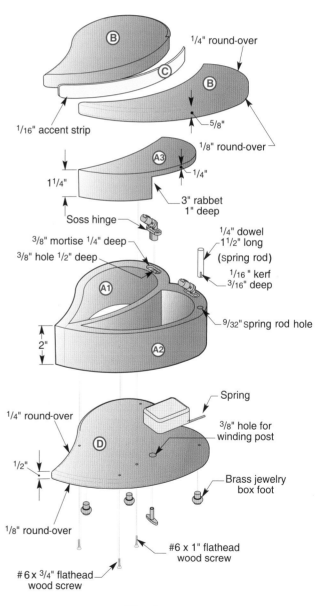

1/4" round-over

1/16" accent strip

1/8" round-over

5/8"

1 1/4"

Soss hinge

3/8" mortise 1/4" deep
3/8" hole 1/2" deep

1/4"

3" rabbet
1" deep

1/4" dowel
1 1/2" long
(spring rod)

1/16" kerf
3/16" deep

9/32" spring rod hole

2"

1/4" round-over

1/2"

1/8" round-over

Spring

3/8" hole for winding post

Brass jewelry box foot

#6 x 1" flathead wood screw

#6 x 3/4" flathead wood screw

Fig. 1

6 **USE A SPINDLE SANDER TO SMOOTH THE EDGES OF PARTS A1, A2, AND A3.** For smooth-sanded edges with minimal burning, sweep the workpiece along the spindle and use a light sideways pressure. Use 80 grit to remove saw marks, then switch to 120 for smoother results. Finally, hand-sand with 220 grit.

7 **SMOOTH THE INNER LOWER TIP OF PART A1 BY HAND.** This area is too tight for the spindle sander, so you may need a file and sandpaper stuck with spray adhesive to a flat stick (such as a paint stirring paddle).

8 **CHECK THE FIT OF PARTS A1 AND A2** for a snug glue joint, and sand any correction that's necessary.

9 **GLUE-UP A1 AND A2 TO MAKE THE BOX BODY.** Match the registration marks near the top of these two parts. Avoid excessive clamping pressure that could bend or even break the pieces. Instead of straight clamps, you might want to try a band clamp. See the **Tip Alert** for other clamping suggestions. Let the box body dry thoroughly, then unclamp.

> **TIP ALERT**
>
> If you don't have a band clamp, consider using ¼" x 4" rubber bands. Glue-up the pieces on a flat surface, such as your saw table or workbench, to ensure proper alignment. But first put down a piece of waxed paper to make sure the assembly doesn't stick to the surface.

Use a fence on your bandsaw to help stabilize the stock when resawing it.

Continue working on the box body

1 **RESAW PART A3 TO 1¼" THICK,** and bandsaw a rabbet to form a recess for the music box movement. Refer to **Figure 1** and **Photo B**. This surface won't be visible, so there's no need to smooth away the saw marks.

2 **WRAP THE EDGE OF PART A3** with pressure-sensitive white birch veneer edgebanding (see the **Convenience-Plus Buying Guide** on page 11). First, run one strip along the inside curve, with the upper edge of the banding a scant ¹⁄₁₆" above the surface of part A3. Press the banding down firmly with a small roller or your fingertips. Cut the ends flush to the wood with a utility knife or veneer saw, then run another strip along the outer curve, and trim its ends flush.

Test-fit part A3 into its recess: You're aiming for a smoothly sliding fit. Sand the edgebanding with 150-grit paper as needed. Wrap the paper around a block and sand off the edgebanding above the top face of A3, making it flush.

3 **CHUCK A ¹⁹⁄₃₂" BIT INTO YOUR DRILL PRESS,** and drill through the box body where shown on the full-sized pattern (page 12). You'll also notice dashed lines on the pattern connecting the hole you just drilled with the

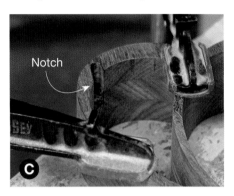

Chisel a notch on the bottom edge to house the spring wire that turns the music box movement on and off.

right-hand cavity in the box body. Chisel out a notch in this channel, as shown in **Photo C**, about 1" deep from the bottom of the box body, for the on/off spring wire of the music-box movement.

Construct the lid

1 **THICKNESS-PLANE A ⅝" THICK BLANK FOR THE LID (B),** and rip and crosscut it approximately 8½" square. Spray-adhere one of the lid/base patterns from page 13 to the bottom of the blank.

2 **BANDSAW THE BLANK INTO TWO PIECES,** steering your blade down the center of the twin dashed lines that show the position of the inlay (C).

3 **SAND THE SAWN EDGES SMOOTH** using your spindle sander. Check the fit of the edges against each other until they meet without a gap. After you've sanded away the saw marks, clamp one of the pieces to your bench. With spray adhesive, stick a strip of 80-grit sandpaper to the cut edge. Lay the other piece next to it, and rub its edge against the sandpaper to smooth its edge to a mating surface. Keep your strokes fairly short—about an inch or so—and regularly blow away the dust to maintain an aggressive cutting action. Remove the sandpaper to check the fit. If the joint needs further work, adhere the sandpaper to the opposite piece and repeat the process.

4 **THICKNESS-PLANE A BLANK ¹¹⁄₁₆" THICK** and at least 12" long for inlay (C). Ensure that the edges of the blank are parallel to each other, and joint both of them straight and smooth. Set up your tablesaw to rip the thin strip from the blank as shown in **Photo D**.

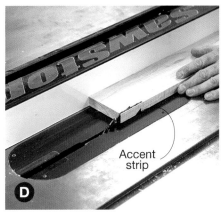

D

Using a 4" wide or wider blank for safe ripping, cut a ¹⁄₁₆" strip, letting the piece fall away from the blank at the end of the cut.

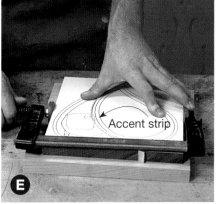

E

Accent strip

With the lid assembly flat, apply the clamping pressure to close the joint and sandwich the accent strip.

F

With the face of the lid up, and against a stopblock, shave the strip flush with the surface.

5 DRY-ASSEMBLE (NO GLUE) THE INLAY (C) between the two halves of the lid (B). Mark the strip's length and cut it. Do one more dry assembly, clamping firmly to make sure that the joint closes cleanly.

6 SPREAD GLUE ON ALL OF THE JOINT SURFACES, and clamp together the lid (B) and inlay (C) as shown in **Photo E**, aligning the registration marks on the pattern. In addition to sideways pressure, you may also need to clamp the pieces to your workbench to ensure that they cannot slide against each other. Also, make certain that the inlay doesn't slide upward. Let the assembly rest until the glue sets.

7 FLUSH THE INLAY (C) TO THE LID (B). Remove most of the waste with a razor-sharp block plane as shown in **Photo F**, or card scraper, then sand it flush.

> **TIP ALERT**
> If the pattern doesn't strip away cleanly, use a cabinet scraper to remove the paper. You can dissolve excess glue with lacquer thinner on a rag. Repeat the wiping several times to lift adhesive residue from the pores of the wood.

8 BANDSAW THE LID ASSEMBLY TO SHAPE, sawing just to the waste side of the line. Don't sand it yet. Instead, put the lid assembly face down on your workbench (with the pattern facing up). Place the box body face down onto the lid assembly (with the pattern facing down). Check that the lid has a consistent overhang of approximately ³⁄₁₆" all around the box body. If necessary, pencil any corrections onto the lid assembly, then spindle-sand the edge of the lid. Strip away the lid pattern (page 13), referring to the **Tip Alert** for clean-up advice.

Make the base

1 THICKNESS-PLANE A BLANK FOR THE BASE (D) TO ½" THICK, and rip and crosscut it 8½" square.

2 JOIN THE LID (B) AND THE BASE BLANK (D) FACE-TO-FACE with double-faced carpet tape. Remove most of the waste by bandsawing to within ¹⁄₈" of the cutline.

3 CHUCK A FLUSH-TRIM RUNNING BIT INTO YOUR TABLE-MOUNTED ROUTER, and rotate the lid/base blank assembly counter-clockwise against the bit to trim away the excess material from the base blank. The bit won't be able to reach into the sharp point of the V to complete the cut, so mark this edge with a pencil.

4 SEPARATE THE LID (B) AND BASE (D). Refer to the **Tip Alert** for help. Complete the shaping of the base's edge with a utility knife or chisel, followed by sanding.

> **TIP ALERT**
> Pieces joined together with double-faced tape can be tough to pry apart. Try tapping a tapered softwood shim between the parts, or drizzle lacquer thinner into the seam to weaken the tape's bond.

5 CUT ALONG THE OUTLINE OF THE REMAINING PATTERN with scissors, and lightly mist it with spray adhesive to adhere it to the bottom of the base (D). Drill all the holes where indicated. The walls of the box body are a fairly small target for the screws that attach the base. Instead of relying strictly on the pattern for the location of the holes, you'll find that it's safer to lay the base on your workbench, then center the box body on it. Now trace the walls of the box body onto the base to make sure that the screws will hit their target. Drill the holes from the top side of the base, but countersink them on the bottom.

Use a router to round over the top edge of the base. A laminate trimmer would be even easier to handle for this task.

6 ROUT A ¼" ROUNDOVER AROUND THE TOP EDGE OF THE BASE. Use a handheld router as shown in **Photo G**, or chuck the bit into your table-mounted router. Remove the pattern from the base.

7 ROUT THE TOP EDGE OF THE LID (B) with the ¼" roundover bit. Switch to a ⅛" roundover bit, and rout both the lid (B) and base (D). Finish-sand all the pieces with 220-grit sandpaper.

Drill for the hinges

1 CHUCK A ⅜" DIAMETER FORSTNER BIT INTO YOUR DRILL PRESS, and set it for a ¼" deep hole for the hinge mortises into the box body (A). See the **Buying Guide** for more on this bit. All of the hinge mortise centerpoints lie along a single line, so you can set up a fence, as shown in **Photo H**, to help ensure consistent results. Drill only the two outer- and inner-most holes for each hinge at this time.

Fence

Set up your drill-press fence to align the hinge mortise centerpoints. This is crucial for smooth hinge operation.

2 PUT DOWEL CENTERS INTO THE FOUR HOLES (see the **Buying Guide** for this inexpensive but handy accessory). The center may not fully seat up to its rim, but don't worry about that. Use a strip of masking tape for each pair of centers to ensure that they won't fall out when you invert the box body.

3 PLACE THE LID (B) FACE DOWN ON YOUR WORKBENCH, and center the inverted box body on it. Lightly tap the box body so that the dowel centers transfer their marks to the lid. Don't overdo the tapping pressure: You want a distinct but small mark as the target for the tip of your drill bit.

4 DRAW A THIN PENCIL LINE CONNECTING EACH PAIR OF MARKS. This will help you accurately position the drill bit for the deeper center holes.

5 REMOVE THE DOWEL CENTERS, and drill the ½" deep center holes into the box body (A). Tap a ½" chisel straight downward to complete the edge of the hinge mortises in the box body. Test-fit the hinges, and clean up the mortises as shown in **Photo I**.

Clean up the hinge mortises with a chisel so that the hinge edge fits closely and the hinge sits flush to the surrounding wood.

6 DRILL AND CHISEL THE HINGE MORTISES into the lid (B), using the same procedures you used for the box body. Be very careful with the ½" depth setting for the center hole because the lid is only ⅝" thick.

7 TEMPORARILY INSTALL THE HINGES into the lid, drilling ⁷⁄₆₄" pilot holes for the supplied screws. Check the action of the hinges.

Begin the assembly

1 CENTER THE BOX BODY (A) ONTO THE BASE (D), and clamp these parts together. Using the countersunk shank holes as guides, drill ⁷⁄₆₄" pilot holes ⅜" deep into the box body. Drive the #6 × ¾" screws to secure the base.

2 TEST-FIT THE MUSIC BOX MOVEMENT into the box body (A), and trim the spring arm with wire cutters to fit into the channel notch below the spring rod hole. Also ensure that the winding post is centered in the hole in the base (D). Drill ⁷⁄₆₄" pilot holes, and screw the movement to the base with two #4 × ½" screws.

3 CUT A ³⁄₁₆" DEEP KERF INTO THE END OF A ¼" DOWEL, where shown in **Figure 1**, using a fine dovetail saw. Fit the dowel into the spring rod hole, engaging the kerf with the spring arm on the music box movement. With the lid open and no downward pressure on the rod, wind the movement and let it play. Slowly press down on the rod until the movement stops completely. Make a pencil mark on the dowel ¹⁄₁₆" above the surface of the box body. Cut the dowel to length, and re-insert it to check its action.

4 REMOVE THE HINGES AND MOVEMENT, and inspect the wood pieces, doing any touch-up sanding necessary.

Apply the finish

1 APPLY A GENEROUS COAT OF DANISH OIL to all of the wood parts, including inside the cavities of the box body (A). Don't forget to finish the dowel. Let the oil soak in for about two minutes, then wipe off all you can with dry cloths. Let dry for two hours.

2 MAKE A ONE-POUND CUT OF SHELLAC by mixing three fluid ounces of denatured alcohol with two fluid ounces of liquid shellac (see the **Buying Guide**). Using a 1" natural-bristle brush, apply three coats of shellac, waiting 30 minutes between coats. Shellac dries fast, so try to flow it onto the surface quickly, with minimum brushing. Let the finish dry overnight.

3 SMOOTH THE SHELLAC BY LIGHTLY SANDING with 400-grit and then 600-grit sandpaper. Use a light touch, and inspect your paper frequently.

4 APPLY A THIN COAT OF WAX, avoiding the surfaces to be flocked. Buff with a soft cloth.

Apply the flocking and reassemble

1 MARK THE LARGE COMPARTMENT ON THE BASE, and remove the base from the box. Unscrew the movement cover (A3). While the directions for the flocking adhesive state that it should be applied to a finished surface, it will stick provided you scuff the marked area and the top face of part A3—both of which receive flocking—with 120-grit sandpaper.

2 FILL THE MINI FLOCK APPLICATOR halfway with black suede flocking (see the **Buying Guide**).

K

Apply the flocking to the special colored adhesive using the Mini Flocker Applicator.

3 APPLY THE FLOCKING ADHESIVE with a 1" foam brush on the surfaces to be flocked. Immediately wipe up any that strays onto unwanted areas with a dry paper towel.

4 GENTLY PUMP THE HANDLE OF THE MINI FLOCK APPLICATOR as shown in **Photo K** to puff the material onto the adhesive. Let dry overnight.

5 REMOVE EXCESS FLOCKING by shaking the parts and lightly wiping with a clean brush.

6 REPLACE THE MUSIC BOX MOVEMENT and base. Next, attach part A3 by positioning it, and using the shank hole in the base (D) as a guide to drill a pilot hole. Drive the screw to secure the part. Epoxy the feet into the base, and replace the hinges and dowel. Don't forget to wind the movement before wrapping the box as a gift. 🦔

Convenience-*PLUS* BUYING GUIDE

	ITEM
☐ 1.	Suede Flocking, Black, 3 oz.
☐ 2.	Suede-Tex Flocking Adhesive, Black, 8 oz
☐ 3.	Mini Flocker Applicator
☐ 4.	Watco Danish Oil, Natural, 1 pt
☐ 5.	Bulls Eye Amber Shellac, 1 qt
☐ 6.	Clear Briwax, 16 oz
☐ 7.	Brusso Jewelry Box Feet, Pack of 4
☐ 8.	SOSS Invisible Hinges, $^3/_8$" x 1", 2
☐ 9.	Denatured Alcohol, 1 qt
☐ 10.	Dowel Centers, $^3/_8$", Pack of 10
☐ 11.	5/64" Vix Bit for #3 & #4 Screws
☐ 12.	7/64" Vix Bit for #5 & #6 Screws
☐ 13.	9/32" Five Star HSS Drill Bit
☐ 14.	#6 x 1" Brass Flathead Wood Screws, 5
☐ 15.	#6 x ¾" Flathead Wood Screws, 2
☐ 16.	Fastedge Peel & Stick Edge Banding, $^{15}/_{16}$" x 8'
☐ 17.	18-Note Standard Music Movement with Spring (sold separately-call (423) 639-5850 to order)

Item above available at: giftsonline.net/catalog_Music_Box_Movements.html

Cutting Diagram

Ⓐ Ⓐ Ⓐ Ⓑ Ⓓ

1" x 10" x 45" Padauk

Ⓒ

1" x 2" x 12" Curly maple

PATTERNS

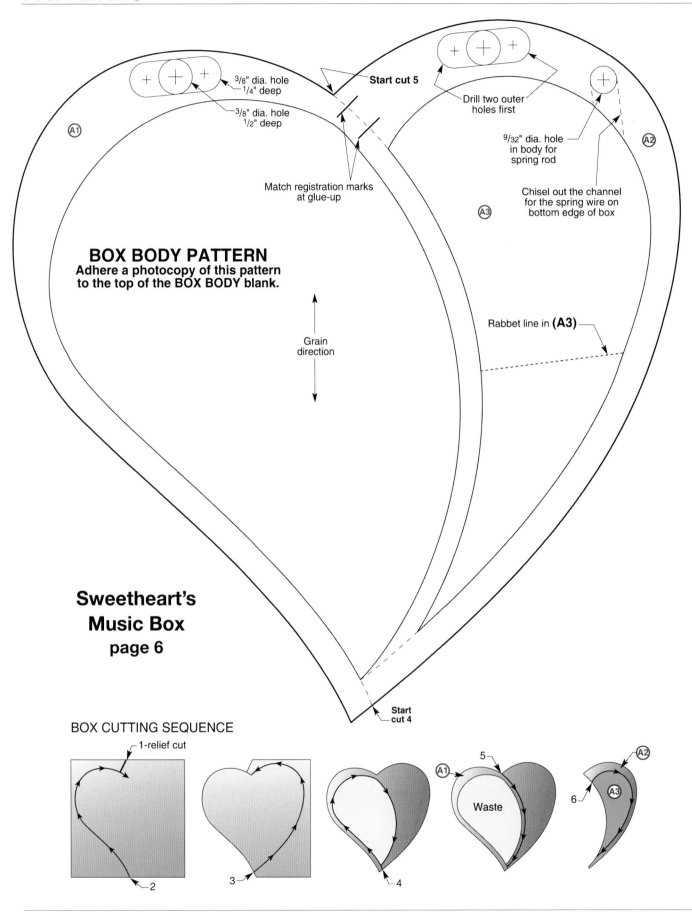

3/8" dia. hole
1/4" deep

3/8" dia. hole
1/2" deep

Start cut 5

Drill two outer holes first

9/32" dia. hole in body for spring rod

Chisel out the channel for the spring wire on bottom edge of box

A1

A2

A3

Match registration marks at glue-up

BOX BODY PATTERN
Adhere a photocopy of this pattern to the top of the BOX BODY blank.

Grain direction

Rabbet line in **(A3)**

Sweetheart's Music Box
page 6

Start cut 4

BOX CUTTING SEQUENCE

1-relief cut

2

3

4

5

6

A1

A2

A3

Waste

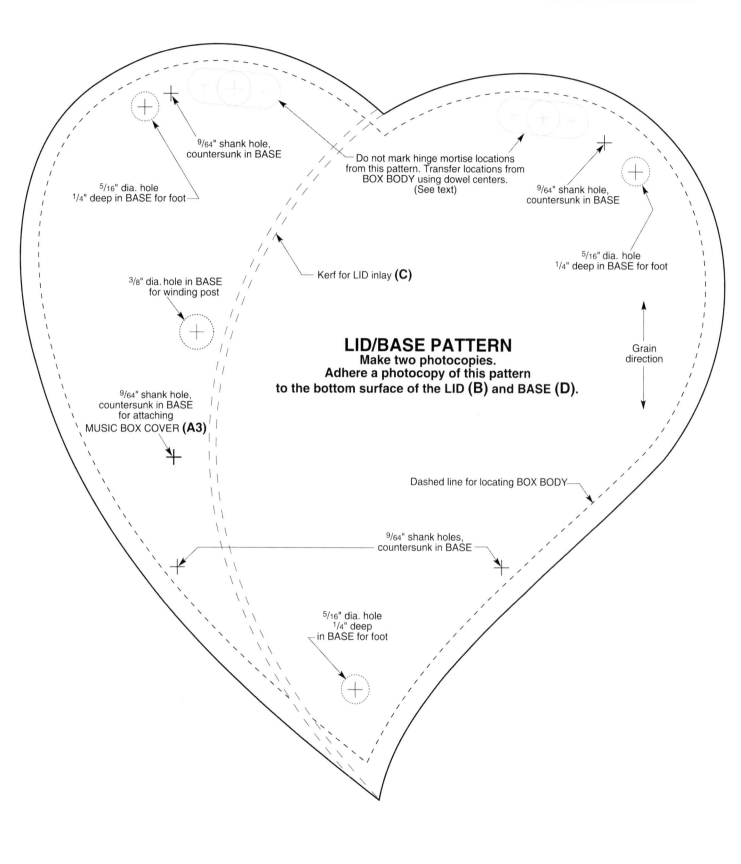

9/64" shank hole,
countersunk in BASE

5/16" dia. hole
1/4" deep in BASE for foot

Do not mark hinge mortise locations
from this pattern. Transfer locations from
BOX BODY using dowel centers.
(See text)

9/64" shank hole,
countersunk in BASE

5/16" dia. hole
1/4" deep in BASE for foot

3/8" dia. hole in BASE
for winding post

Kerf for LID inlay **(C)**

Grain
direction

LID/BASE PATTERN
Make two photocopies.
Adhere a photocopy of this pattern
to the bottom surface of the LID (B) and BASE (D).

9/64" shank hole,
countersunk in BASE
for attaching
MUSIC BOX COVER **(A3)**

Dashed line for locating BOX BODY

9/64" shank holes,
countersunk in BASE

5/16" dia. hole
1/4" deep
in BASE for foot

SPLINED KEEPSAKE BOX

Build a keepsake container in treasured wood.

By Paul Anthony

Overall dimensions: 12¾"w × 6¾"d × 4⅜"h

This beautiful box, with its spline-reinforced mitered corners, makes a great gift for that special person. Part of its beauty is that it's easy to build and lets you display that stunning piece of figured wood you stashed way for just the right project.

I used walnut for the box, and spalted sycamore for the top panel, bottom, and keys. Simple routed moldings serve as the feet.

I built the box as an enclosed unit of only six pieces: the four sides, top, and bottom. After assembling the box and cutting the

key slots in the sides with the top and bottom in place, I sawed off the lid, then routed the coved recess for the finger lift. I attached the feet, then secured the lid with a pair of quality brass hinges. Inside, I added a removable tray. *See the **Convenience-Plus Buying Guide** on page 19 for supplies.*

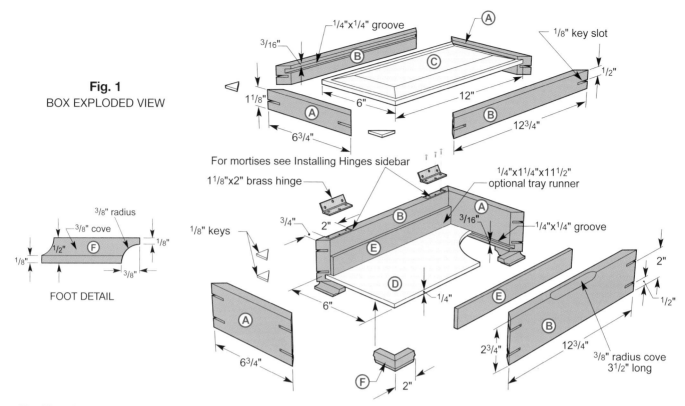

Fig. 1
BOX EXPLODED VIEW

1/4"x1/4" groove

3/16"

1/8" key slot

1/2"

1 1/8"

6"

12"

6 3/4"

12 3/4"

For mortises see Installing Hinges sidebar

1 1/8"x2" brass hinge

1/8" keys

3/4"

2"

1/4"x1 1/4"x11 1/2"
optional tray runner

3/16"

1/4"x1/4" groove

2"

1/2"

6"

1/4"

2 3/4"

12 3/4"

3/8" radius cove
3 1/2" long

3/8" radius

3/8" cove

1/8"

1/2"

1/8"

3/8"

1/8"

FOOT DETAIL

6 3/4"

2"

Build the basic box

1 LAY OUT THE STOCK (see the **Cutting Diagram** on page 19) for the ends (A) and sides (B) in sequence on one long board to create continuous "wrap-around" grain that terminates at a back corner. This also keeps the stock long enough for safe handling when milling. Thickness-plane the board to ⅝" and rip it to 4⅛" wide, allowing an extra foot or so for tool setups later. Mill pieces for the top (C) and bottom (D) panels to their respective thicknesses and cut them to length and width (see the **Cut List** on page 19).

Crosscut the sides to length, sand smooth the inside faces, then set up to miter the ends of the pieces on the tablesaw. Cut a test piece to ensure your blade cuts at exactly 45° and that your miter gauge is adjusted for a perfect 90° cut. Then miter-cut the box ends (A) and sides (B) as shown in **Photo A**.

2 SAW THE GROOVES for the top and bottom where shown in **Figure 1**, insetting them ³⁄₁₆" from the top and bottom edges of box ends (A) and sides (B). Use a dado set, or two passes with a standard saw blade.

> **TIP ALERT**
> Before crosscutting sequential pieces from a board to create wrap-around grain, make sure to mark adjacent ends for repositioning later.

3 OUTFIT YOUR ROUTER TABLE with a panel-raising bit. At a reduced speed, rout the profile in ½" thick scrap to make sure it yields the shape you want and that the edges seat fully in the routed grooves. Then rout the profile on the top face of the top panel, taking incremental passes for safety as shown in **Photo B**. For the cleanest result, make a light final pass.

A

Hold the stock firmly against the saw table when sawing miters, and use a stop to ensure accuracy.

B

Use a featherboard to hold the top panel against the router table. A backerboard stabilizes the piece.

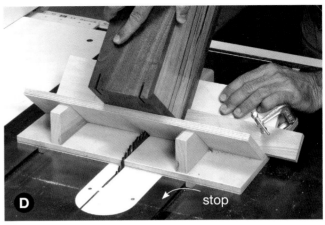

C Do a dry clamp-up before gluing—using band clamps allows you to check the fit of the joints and panels and to rehearse your clamping procedure.

D Cut the spline slots by holding the box firmly in a cradle jig while pushing it across the blade. A stop in the miter gauge slot prevents overtravel here.

4 SAND THE TOP AND BOTTOM PANELS to 220 grit, then apply several coats of finish to both. (I used shellac because it's easy to apply, dries quickly, and won't trap an offensive odor inside the box. Wipe a ½" band of shellac on the inside faces adjacent to the miter joints. This will ease removal of interior glue squeeze-out later.

Dry-clamp the sides together with the top and bottom in their grooves **(Photo C)**. Check the fit of the joints and trim the edges of the top and bottom panels if necessary. Remember to leave ¹⁄₁₆" of room for any cross-grain expansion during the humid season.

Glue the sides together with band clamps. (Don't glue the panels in their grooves.) After the glue cures, clean up any exterior squeeze-out. With a smoothing plane, scraper, or sanding block, smooth the top and bottom edges flush, as well as the corners, if necessary, to remove any jutting or slightly offset mitered edges.

> **TIP ALERT**
> Always finish a solid wood panel before installing it in its frame to prevent exposing raw wood when the panel shrinks in the dry season.

Spline the corners with keys

1 TO SAW THE CORNER SLOTS FOR THE KEY SPLINES, you'll need to guide the box sides at a 45° angle over your tablesaw blade. To do this, build the corner splining jig shown in **Figure 2**. It includes a blade-guard block on the trailing end of the jig for safety.

2 TO USE THE JIG TO CUT SLOTS, raise the blade to cut just shy of ¾" deep into the box corner. For quick, consistent slots all around, clamp a stopblock to the cradle ½" away from the blade, then cut all eight of the outer slots. Cut into the jig only as far as needed to saw the box corners, and not completely through the jig's base.

Next, adjust the stop and cut the center slots 2" up from the box bottom as shown in **Photo D**.

> **TIP ALERT**
> To avoid slots with V-shaped bottoms, use an ATBR (alternate top bevel with raker teeth) combination blade to cut a square-bottomed slot.

Fig. 2
CORNER SPLINING JIG

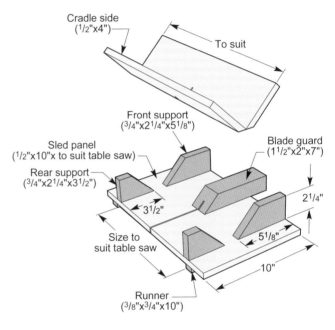

Cradle side (½"x4")

To suit

Front support (¾"x2¼"x5⅛")

Blade guard (1½"x2"x7")

Sled panel (½"x10"x to suit table saw)

Rear support (¾"x2¼"x3½")

3½"

2¼"

Size to suit table saw

5⅛"

10"

Runner (⅜"x¾"x10")

3 MILL A STRIP OF ⅞" WIDE STOCK for the splines, sawing or planing it for a snug fit in the slots. Then saw the individual keys to shape as shown in **Photo E**, making them about ¼" oversized in length. Test-fit the keys in their slots, sanding any that are too tight. Then glue the keys in, seating them firmly in their slots.

4 TRIM THE KEYS FLUSH with the box ends and sides. To do this quickly, attach ¼" thick hardboard to the box sides with double-faced tape. Then outfit your table-mounted router with a ¼" straight bit and cut just a hair proud of the surrounding wood as shown in **Photo F**. A random-orbit sander or a few quick swipes inward from the corners with a sharp, finely set block plane, finishes the job.

Register the strip of spline stock against a setup block on the rip fence, holding the thin material down with a stick. After making the cut, flip the strip over and repeat for the next cut.

Cut away the lid and hinge it in place

1 SET YOUR TABLESAW FENCE for a 2⅞" rip and raise the blade ¾". With the box bottom against the fence, rip away the box top. After sawing through the box ends and one side, shim the saw kerf to maintain its width before making the final cut shown in **Photo G**. Afterward, plane or sand the sawn edges smooth and clean up any glue squeeze-out from the inside corners using a blade removed from a block plane.

2 USING A ⅜" RADIUS COVE BIT, rout the 3½" long by ⁷⁄₁₆" high finger lift recess. Set up stopblocks on the fence to establish the cut length. After test-cutting in scrap, rout the cove in several passes as shown in **Photo H**, taking a light final pass to minimize burning.

3 INSTALL A QUALITY PAIR of 1⅛" × 2" drawn-brass butt hinges by mortising out recesses for each leaf as described in "Installing Butt Hinges" on page 18, then screw the hinges in place.

4 PLANE AND CUT TWO PIECES of stock to ¼" × 1¼" × 11½" for the tray supports (E). Glue and clamp them in place where shown in **Figure 1**.

5 WITH THE LID HINGED and clamped to the box, plane, scrape, and/or sand the box assembly flush all around. Remove the hinges and sand the lid and box to 220 grit.

Make the feet

Note: The small pieces for the feet would be difficult to machine individually. A safer way to make the feet is to build a small coved frame, and then cut the four feet from the frame corners.

1 MILL FOUR PIECES of ½" × ¾" × 6" stock for the frame, then miter the ends and glue up the frame. After the glue cures, plane or sand the faces and edges of the frame.

With the box riding on hardboard scraps, trim the splines just shy of the box surface with a straight bit.

After sawing through the box ends and one side, use tape to clamp the shims in the saw kerf, ensuring a safe, clean cut upon separation.

When routing the lift cove, place the box against the right-hand stopblock, pivot it against the fence, and then move the box toward the left-hand stop.

Rout the cove on the feet by standing the frame on edge on the router table. A featherboard ensures accuracy and safety during the cut.

Cutting the corners to length is quickly and safely done with a tablesaw sled and stopblock. Hold the pieces down with a scrap block.

Clamp the foot to a block to steady it when cutting the end coves on a scrollsaw.

2 INSTALL A ⅜" RADIUS COVE BIT in a table-mounted router with the cutting edge projecting ¼" above the table. Rout the cove with the frame standing on edge as shown in **Photo I**. Then sand the cove to 220 grit using sandpaper wrapped around a ¾" diameter dowel.

3 CROSSCUT 2" LONG CORNERS from the frame to create the feet (F). For safety, use a crosscut sled on the tablesaw as shown in **Photo J**. Alternatively, you could cut them with a handsaw.

4 MARK THE ⅜" COVE on the inside ends of each foot (see Foot Detail in **Figure 1**). Tracing around a ¾" diameter dowel

works well for this. Then cut the cove with a scrollsaw as shown in **Photo K**, and clean it up with a sandpaper-wrapped dowel. Sand the feet to 220 grit, and then glue them to the box bottom, aligning the inside faces of the feet with the inside edges of the box walls.

Build the tray and finish up

1 PLANE A 1⅛" × 24" PIECE OF WALNUT to ¼" thick for the tray sides (G, H). Cut the ⅛" groove ⅛" deep for the tray bottom (I), and then miter-cut four sides to length. Scrollsaw and sand the notches in parts (H) where shown in **Figure 3**.

INSTALLING BUTT HINGES

Neatly installed butt hinges make an enormous difference in the look of a box or cabinet. Slow, careful work and a systematic approach is all it takes. Here's how to do it.

Lay out the mortises on the back edge of the box where shown in **Figure 1**, aligning each hinge pin centerline with the rear edge of the box. Lightly knife along the short ends of a hinge, then deepen the lines by guiding the knife against a small square. Set a marking gauge equal to the distance between the centerpoint of the hinge barrel and outside edge of one leaf, then scribe the long edge of each mortise.

Install a ¼" straight router bit in your handheld router and adjust it to project just a hair shy of the hinge pin centerpoint. Set a router edge guide to cut to the rear of the mortise. Rout the mortises to within ¹⁄₁₆" or so from your end scribe lines as shown in the photo at right. Afterward, slice away at the remaining waste with a razor-sharp chisel, inserting it in the knife line for each final cut.

Clamp the box lid over the folded hinges and use a sharp knife to nick the lid at the ends of each hinge. Align a square with each nick and extend a deep knife line across the lid edge to scribe the ends of the hinge mortises. Use the previously set marking gauge to scribe the long edge, then rout and chisel out the mortise.

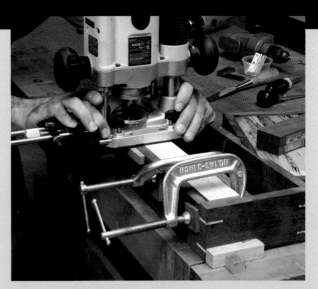

CLAMP A SHORT BOARD to the box wall to support the base of the router. Use an edge guide to rout the long rear wall of the mortise.

2 PLANE A PIECE OF FIGURED WOOD

for the tray bottom (I) to ¼" thick. Cut it to size and rout a ⅛" rabbet ⅛" deep along the edges. Test-fit the piece in the grooves in the tray sides. Apply glue, then clamp the tray parts together.

3 MARK ½" IN FROM THE CORNERS

on the outside faces of the tray, then using a fine-toothed handsaw, cut down to these lines to create kerfs for the keys. Plane a contrasting wood to the kerf widths and cut the triangular keys to fit. Add glue and insert the keys, trimming them flush after the glue dries. Sand the tray to 220 grit.

4 APPLY SEVERAL COATS of your

favorite finish to the box. I recommend brushing a couple thin coats of shellac on the box interior. Unlike oil or varnish, shellac dries quickly, so the interior of the box won't have a lingering solvent smell. I applied a few coats of wiping varnish to the exterior. Give the finish a day to dry, then rub out the surface with 0000 steel wool and wax. 🐗

Fig. 3
TRAY EXPLODED VIEW

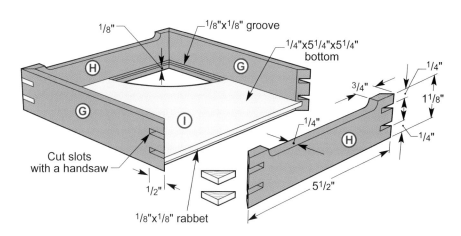

Cut slots with a handsaw

1/8"
1/8"x1/8" groove
1/4"x5¼"x5¼" bottom
1/4"
3/4"
1 1/8"
1/4"
5 1/2"
1/2"
1/8"x1/8" rabbet

Cutting Diagram

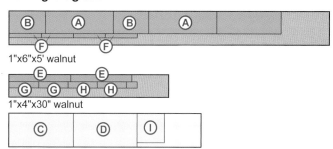

Ⓑ Ⓐ Ⓑ Ⓐ
Ⓕ Ⓕ
1"x6"x5' walnut

Ⓔ Ⓔ
Ⓖ Ⓖ Ⓗ Ⓗ
1"x4"x30" walnut

Ⓒ Ⓓ Ⓘ
1"x6"x36" figured wood

Keepsake Box Cut List		Thickness	Width	Length	Qty.	Mat'l
Box and Lid						
A	Ends	⅝"	4"	6¾"	2	W
B*	Sides	⅝"	4"	12¾"	2	W
C	Lid top	½"	6"	12"	1	FW
D	Box bottom	¼"	6"	12"	1	FW
E	Tray supports	¼"	1¼"	11½"	2	W
F*	Frame for feet	½"	¾"	2×2"	4	W
Tray						
G	Front and back	¼"	1⅛"	5½"	2	W
H	Notched sides	¼"	1⅛"	5½"	2	W
I	Bottom	¼"	5¼"	5¼"	1	FW

*Saw feet from framed corners after assembly.
W=Walnut FW=Figured Wood

When closed the box shows off an exquisite piece of figured wood; in this case, spalted sycamore.

COVED JEWELRY BOX

Sleek, with a slide top, and built totally at the tablesaw

By Geoff Noden

Overall Dimensions: 2½"w × 1⅞"h × 12"l

I like the way a coved pencil tray in a desk drawer allows you to easily scoop out the contents. Borrowing the concept, I designed this sleek jewelry box that occupies very little space on a dresser or desktop. The box is compartmentalized with dividers, which also close off the ends of the cove. I used a sliding lid, beveling it to complement the upward flare on the box sides, as shown in **Figure 1**.

To make this project you need little more than a tablesaw and block of wood. For flat-bottom grooves and rabbets, outfit your saw with a combination blade that includes flat-ground teeth. I'll show you how to make a 2½" wide × 1⅞" high × 12" long cherry box of a certain style from a single block of wood, but you actually have various design options. For example, you can use a complementary wood for

the top and/or dividers. The top can be beveled, left flat, or even augmented with banding or inlay. Once you understand the basic steps of building this particular box, you'll be able to make larger and smaller versions, adjusting your saw setups to suit. For efficiency, consider making multiple boxes at the same time. Believe me, you won't have any problems finding takers for them.

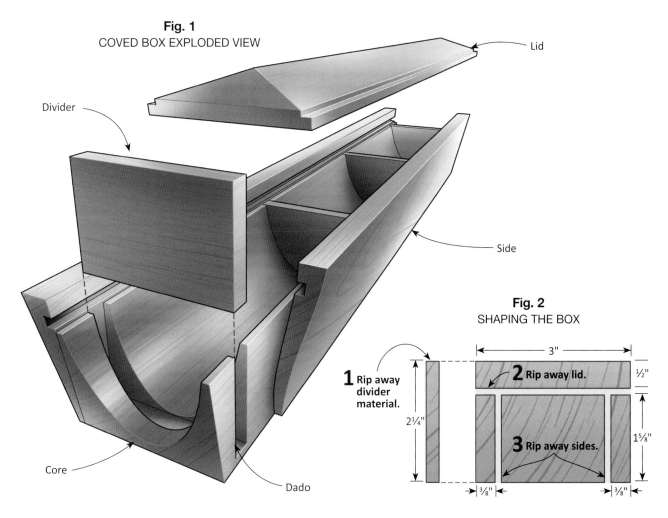

Fig. 1
COVED BOX EXPLODED VIEW

Lid

Divider

Side

Core

Dado

Fig. 2
SHAPING THE BOX

1 Rip away divider material.

3"

2 Rip away lid.

½"

2¼"

3 Rip away sides.

1⅝"

⅜" ⅜"

Lid

1/32" **5** Trim edges.

6 Saw grooves ⅛ × ⅛".

1/16"

Side

4 Saw cove.

⅛" min.

Separate the lid and sides

1 **MILL A BLOCK OF WOOD** to 2¼" thick by 3⅜" × 12", as shown in Figure 2. Rip a strip from one edge that will serve as the divider material. Make it just over ¼" thick, to allow belt sanding or hand-planing later, for a perfect fit into a ¼" dado.

2 **RIP ½" FROM THE MOST ATTRACTIVE FACE** to create the lid. Then rip a ⅜" thick slice from each edge to separate the sides from the core. Holding the sides against the core in their original orientation, draw reference marks across their ends for reassembly later.

Make the cove and grooves

1 **ADJUST YOUR BLADE** so its apex is at the level of your tabletop. Use a protractor and bevel gauge to set up your tablesaw with an angled fence as shown in **Figure 3**; then clamp the fence to your saw table. *Note: This setup will get you pretty close to your target, but you may have to finesse the fence angle as described to fine-tune the cove as you work.*

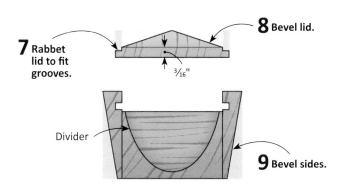

7 Rabbet lid to fit grooves.

8 Bevel lid.

3/16"

Divider

9 Bevel sides.

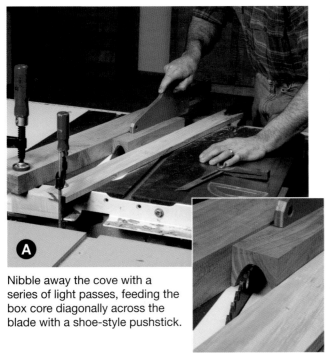

A

Nibble away the cove with a series of light passes, feeding the box core diagonally across the blade with a shoe-style pushstick.

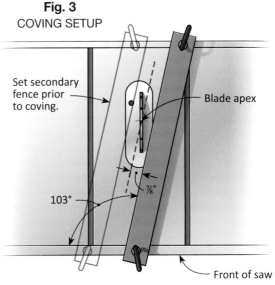

Fig. 3
COVING SETUP

Set secondary fence prior to coving.

Blade apex

103°

⅞"

Front of saw

2 SECURE A SECONDARY FENCE to the table, offsetting it parallel to the primary fence by the width of the box core. Make sure the core slides easily between the fences without side-to-side play.

3 SAW THE COVE by taking a series of light cuts, raising your blade about ¹⁄₁₆" for each pass **(Photo A)**. As you progress, make sure the cove is centered on the core, adjusting the fences if necessary. Continue until either the cove is within ⅛" of the box bottom, or until you've created a ¹⁄₃₂"-wide flat on the peaks of the edges, whichever comes first (see **Figure 2**).

4 SAND THE COVE (see sidebar at right). Then apply two coats of a wiping varnish to the interior and let it dry thoroughly. (You can skip the varnishing if you plan to flock the interior, as discussed in "Flocking" on page 24.)

5 REMOVE THE CLAMPED FENCES, and set your saw's rip fence 1¼" from the blade. Then trim off the peaks at the edges of the cove as shown in **Photo B**.

6 RELOCATE THE RIP FENCE about ¹⁄₃₂" further from the blade, and set the blade height to project ⅛" above the table. Saw the ⅛"× ⅛" grooves for the lid where shown in **Figure 2**, feeding the bottom edge of each side against the rip fence. (The ¹⁄₃₂" offset ensures that the dividers on the completed box won't impede lid operation.)

Create the compartments

1 OUTFIT YOUR SAW WITH A SHARP DADO HEAD configured to make a ¼" wide cut, and locate your rip fence ½" away from the blade. Raise the dado head so the teeth will just lightly graze the bottom of the inverted cove.

A Custom Sanding Block for Coves

To make a custom sanding block for use on a cove, first adhere a sheet of 120-grit sandpaper to the cove using double-faced tape or spray adhesive. Saw a block of rigid insulation to match the width of the cove. Then sand the block to shape as shown.

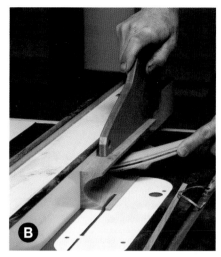

Use pushsticks to hold the coved core safely and securely against the table and fence to trim the peaks.

Using the rip fence as a stop and a miter gauge with an auxiliary fence, saw the divider dadoes with a dado head.

2 MASK THE LEADING HALF OF THE COVE with heavy tape to minimize exit tear-out inside the cove. (I used Gorilla Tape, available at home supply stores.)

3 USING THE RIP FENCE AS A STOP, and the miter gauge to feed the workpiece, cut the outermost dado at each end of the box. Next, adjust the fence 4⅛" from the dado head, and cut the two innermost dadoes **(Photo C)**.

4 CROSSCUT THE DIVIDER STRIP you made earlier into pieces about ¼" longer than the width of the core. Then adjust the thickness of each piece individually for a perfect fit into its dado. (I used double-faced tape to attach a small wooden cube to each divider. Using the cube as a grip, I pressed the divider against an inverted belt sander clamped in a vise.)

5 GLUE THE DIVIDERS into their dadoes, roughly centered. Let the glue dry.

6 MAKE A NOTCHED FEEDER BOARD as shown in **Photo D**; then trim the sides and divider ends down, adjusting the rip fence as needed to create a ¹⁄₁₆" flat at the top edges of the cove.

7 SMOOTH THE OUTER EDGES OF THE CORE and the interior faces of the box sides, using a hand plane or 220-

grit sandpaper backed by a hardwood block. Then glue the sides to the core, carefully aligning the bottom edges of the pieces **(Photo E)**.

Make the lid

1 MEASURE THE DISTANCE BETWEEN THE BOTTOMS of the mating lid grooves, subtract about ¹⁄₁₆", and rip the lid to that width.

2 WITH THE INVERTED LID LYING FLAT on the saw table, cut the rabbet on each edge. Aim for a snug, but easy sliding fit in the box grooves.

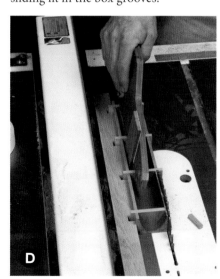

Trim the edges of the core using a notched board. A tab taped to the pusher applies side pressure.

Glue the sides to the core, clamping down across the dividers to press the core flat to the assembly table.

3 SET YOUR TABLESAW BLADE ANGLE at 10°. With the ends of the installed lid aligned with the ends of the box, tape and hold the parts firmly together while crosscutting each end of the box.

4 MAKE A JIG like that shown in **Photo F**. Angle your saw blade to 20°, and set up the cut using a piece of ½" thick scrap. Adjust the rip fence to yield a bevel that leaves a ³⁄₁₆" wide flat on the end of the scrap (see **Figure 2**). Then saw the bevels on the ends of the lid.

F

Bevel the ends of the lid using an L-shaped board with a vertical fence to support the workpiece at 90°.

G

To bevel the lid edges, tape the workpiece to a carrier board. (Note that I am feeding from the left of the saw.)

5 TO SAFELY SAW THE BEVELS **ALONG THE LENGTH** of the lid, make a carrier board as shown in **Photo G**. Then, making test cuts, creep up on the final setting by adjusting the fence location to avoid sawing into the tongue at the edge of the lid. Aim to leave enough material so that a final cleanup with sandpaper or a hand plane yields a neat intersection at the corners of the lid where the adjacent bevels meet. After sawing the first bevel, remove the lid from the jig, reattach it at 180°, and saw the opposite one.

6 HAND-PLANE and/or sand the lid to clean up the bevels.

7 RESET YOUR BLADE ANGLE to 10°, and rip the bevel on each side of the box.

8 SAND THE BOX THROUGH 220 grit. Smooth the ends with the lid installed to maintain the proper angle at the ends of the lid.

Finish up

Apply your choice of finish. I used three coats of wipe-on polyurethane varnish. Top it off with a coat of wax for a lustrous finish and smooth lid operation. 🪚

Flocking

Flocking the interior of a box softens and dresses it up while eliminating the necessity of applying finish to the cove. To apply flocking, first paint on a coat of adhesive, using the same color as the flocking. Then dump the flocking into the box, close the lid, and shake it well. Let it dry for a day, and then tap out and gently blow off the excess, which can be used for your next project.

Overall dimensions:
19¼"w × 12¼"d × 13⅞"h

COLLECTOR'S SHOWCASE

Display your treasures in style in this handsome glass-topped box.
By Craig Bentzley

Box projects are perennial favorites with woodworkers. They're a fun way to hone your skills, and there's always a need for additional storage. While extra storage is appreciated, the treasures within are usually unseen. This good-looking tabletop showcase is different. Sporting a glass top and four interchangeable drawers, this case serves as a mini-museum. It offers up an ever-changing display that makes collections easy to see while keeping them secure.

In addition to showing off your favorite keepsakes, this box gives you an opportunity to display your woodworking skills. You'll get a chance to try your hand at simple veneering, using rail-and-stile bits, installing full-mortise locks, cutting interlocking drawer dividers, and lining drawers. In the end, you'll have an heirloom quality piece suited to any décor.
Note: For a list of the materials and supplies used to build this box, see the **Convenience-Plus Buying Guide** *on page 32.*

25

Fig. 1
COLLECTOR'S SHOWCASE
EXPLODED VIEW

$9^3/_{16}$ x $16^3/_{16}$"
tempered glass

SIDE PANEL DETAIL

$12^1/_4$" $19^1/_4$"

$1^1/_8$" mini-biscuit

$1/_4$" radius cove

$1/_2$" rabbet, $1/_4$" deep

$11^1/_2$"

$3/_4$" rabbet, $1/_2$" deep

$1/_2$"

$2^1/_4$"

$1/_2$"

$2^1/_4$"

$1/_2$"

$11^3/_4$"

$1/_2$" dadoes, $1/_4$" deep

$2^1/_4$"

$1/_2$"

$2^1/_4$"

$3/_4$"

$3/_4$"

$3/_4$" rabbet, $1/_4$" deep

$3/_4$"

$3/_4$" rabbet, $1/_4$" deep

Trim exposed $1^1/_8$" mini-biscuit

Veneer

Cut $1/_8$" wide x $3/_8$" deep slot $3/_8$" from front edge.

17"

10"

$1/_4$" rabbet $3/_8$" deep

$19^1/_4$"

1"

R=$11/_16$"

$1^1/_2$"

$12^1/_4$"

$1/_4$" radius cove

Make the veneered panels

Veneering the side and back panels to match the curly maple drawer fronts is a simpler and less expensive alternative to using solid wood. Despite the conventional wisdom that panels must be balanced on both sides, these panels are only veneered on the show face. By using a ¼" Baltic birch substrate and containing the panel within the rails and stiles, the small panel is neither willing nor able to move.

1 TO CREATE A SIMPLE VENEER PRESS, make a pair of ¾" × 8" × 16" clamping cauls. (I used melamine because it's cheap and most glues won't stick to it.) Also make three pairs of bearers from 2" × 3" construction lumber. Plane a slight crown along the length of the bearers to direct extra pressure to the center of the sandwich when applying clamps to the ends.

Transparent tape

Apply a few tabs of tape to keep the veneer from shifting. An expired credit card, cut with pinking shears, makes an efficient glue spreader.

2 CUT THE SIDE AND BACK PANELS approximately ¼" larger than the finished sizes in the **Cut List** (page 32). The extra material provides insurance against veneer shift during glue-up. Using the plywood panels as guides, cut the veneer to size with a utility knife or veneer saw.

3 WORKING ONE PANEL at a time, tape the long edge of the veneer to the underside of the substrate and spread glue on the top face of the plywood as shown in **Photo A**. Fold the veneer onto the panel, attach tape to the free edge, and then use a roller to work out bubbles and spread the excess glue.

Crowned bearers direct extra clamping pressure to the middle of the glue-up. Clamping the center bearer first helps force excess glue out to the edges.

Hold down the panel firmly and trim one edge. To decrease the chance of chipping the veneer, orient the panels so the good side faces up.

4 PLACE THE VENEERED PANEL between the cauls and arrange the bearers as shown in **Photo B**. Clamp the ends of the bearers and then place a few extra clamps around the edges. Allow time to dry.

5 REPEAT STEPS 1-3 with the two remaining panels. When you're done, use a cabinet scraper to remove tape and dried glue. Finish-sand the good veneered face through 220 grit.

6 MOISTURE IN THE GLUE will make the veneer swell a bit, creating some overhang. Using a tablesaw and crosscut sled, as shown in **Photo C**, butt an end against the fence and true one long edge of each panel. Now cut the panels to final size for side panels (A) and back panel (B).

7 IF YOU WANT TO ENHANCE THE LOOK of the figured panels, but don't intend to color the entire project, stain the veneered panels now, then put them aside.

> **TIP ALERT**
> Routing rails and stiles will require some test cuts. Mill extra stock so that you can fine-tune your bit settings.

Make the case

1 MILL THE RAIL AND STILE stock (C-H) to ¾" thick. Referring to the **Cut List**, joint and rip the parts to correct widths, and then crosscut to length.

2 MEASURE THE THICKNESS of your side and back panels (A, B) and

adjust the width of the slot cutters on your rail and stile bits to match. Next, install the rail bit in a table-mounted router. Use a straightedge to align the guide bearing flush with the fence and set the fillet for ¹⁄₁₆". Now cope the ends of the side rails (C, D) and back rails (F, G), as shown in **Photo D**. Make sure to keep the ends of the rails tight against the fence.

3 INSTALL THE STILE BIT in a table-mounted router. Align the guide bearing with the fence and adjust the fillet depth to match the rail. Make a test cut on scrap, and adjust the height as necessary to ensure perfectly flush faces. Now rout the profile on the inside edges of the rail and stile stock (C-H) as shown in **Photo E**.

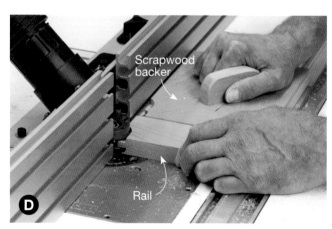

Use a sandpaper-faced backer block to keep the rails from slipping into the fence opening and to prevent blowout at the end of the cut.

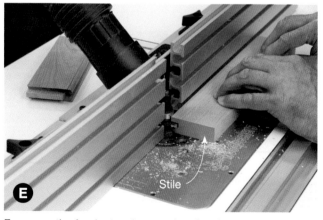

Focus on the feed rate when routing the cherry stiles. Feed quickly enough to prevent burning, but slowly enough to avoid tear-out.

4 ARRANGE THE PARTS according to subassemblies; sides (A, C, D, E) and back (B, F, G, H). The subassemblies go together identically. Apply glue to the stub tenons on a rail and a small amount in each end of the stiles. Insert that rail into the stile, slide in the panel, and then insert the second rail. Now attach the second stile and then press the assembly together.

Lay the assembled panel onto a pair of clamps and apply pressure to the rails. Use a straightedge to make sure that the assemblies are flat and the ends of the stiles are flush with the rails. Repeat the process with the other two panels.

5 MILL THE STOCK for the drawer dividers (I, J), drawer runners (K, L), upper drawer kickers (M), rear screw cleat (N), and lower drawer support (O). Cut the parts to the dimensions on the **Cut List**.

6 INSTALL A DADO SET in your tablesaw and cut the ½" rabbets ¼" deep along the top edge of the side panel assemblies (A, C, D, E) where shown in **Figure 1**. Adjust the fence and cut the dadoes for the drawer runners (K, L)

and drawer dividers (I, J) as shown in **Photo F**. Next, cut the ¾" rabbets ¼" deep along the bottom edge of the side panel assemblies.

7 ROTATE THE SIDE PANEL 90° and cut the ¾" rabbets ¼" deep on the front of the side panel assemblies to house the drawer false fronts (AA) where shown in **Figure 1**. Finally, cut the ¾" rabbets ¼" deep for the back panel assembly (B, F, G, H).

8 APPLY GLUE to the two side assemblies (A, C, D, E), position the back between them, and then apply light clamping pressure to hold the box together. Insert the drawer dividers without glue, as shown in **Photo G** and increase clamping pressure.

9 INSTALL A ⅛" SLOTTING BIT in a table-mounted router, clamp the router table slotting jig (refer to the slotting jig sidebar on page 29) to the fence, and cut ⅛" wide slots to fit mini biscuits on the inside edges of the drawer dividers (I, J), and the ends of the drawer runners (K, L) and kickers (M) where shown in **Figure 1**. Locate the jig so the cutter doesn't break through the visible edges

of the parts. Now, plunge the parts into the rotating bit. Trim the ends of the biscuits so they don't protrude from the outer edges of the parts.

10 USING THE SAME SLOTTING BIT, cut the ⅛" wide mortises ⅜" deep for the lock strikes in all drawer dividers (I, J) where shown in **Figure 1**.

11 DRILL AND COUNTERSINK SCREW holes in the upper drawer divider (I), upper drawer kickers (M), and rear cleat (N) where shown in **Figure 1**.

12 GLUE ALL THE RUNNERS (K, L) and dividers (I, J) into the box. Make and install the four drawer guides (P) where shown in **Figure 1**.

Make the top

1 MILL THE TOP FRAME front/rear (Q) and sides (R) to ⅝" thick. Referring to the **Cut List**, joint and then rip the parts to width. Leave them a few inches long for now.

With a dado set, cut the ½" wide dadoes for the drawer runners and dividers. Use the sacrificial fence to cut the rabbets on the top and bottom edge.

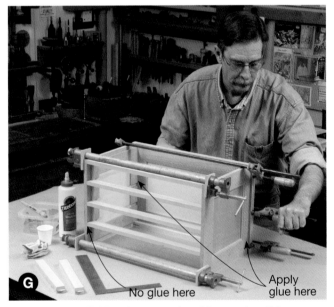

No glue here

Apply glue here

Dry-fitting the dividers between the side panels will keep the box assembly square as you glue and clamp the sides to the back.

This simple jig provides an easy way to support workpieces when slotting square-cut and mitered ends for biscuits or splines. Use it to reinforce the runners (K, L) and kickers (M), and in the mitered top frame parts (Q, R) as shown at right.

After building the jig as shown, set your router table's fence ⅜" in front of the bearing and adjust the bit height to cut a slot at the midpoint of your stock.

When slotting narrow pieces, locate the jig on the fence so that the biscuit will protrude from a less visible edge, for trimming later. When slotting wide pieces, position the jig so the slot is centered on the stock.

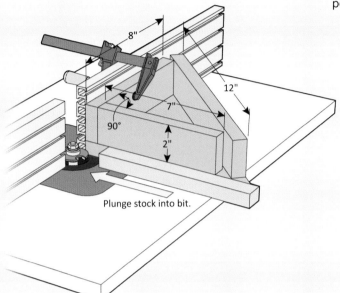

8"
12"
7"
90°
2"

Plunge stock into bit.

2 USING A TABLE-MOUNTED ROUTER, align the guide bearing flush with the fence and set the fillet for ¹⁄₁₆". Shape the inside edges of the top frame's front/rear (Q) and sides (R).

3 SET YOUR TABLESAW BLADE height to ¼" and fence to ¹³⁄₃₂" and rip off the bottom lip of the groove from the top frame parts (Q, R) to create a rabbet for the tempered glass top.

4 WITH A TABLE-MOUNTED ROUTER and ¼" radius cove bit, rout the bottom outside edges of the frame parts (See **Figure 1**).

5 MITER-CUT THE TOP FRAME (front/rear) (Q) and sides (R) to final length. Dry-fit the frame to check the fit of the miters. Use the router table and slotting jig, but this time employ the jig's mitered face, as shown above. Adjust the bit and jig so that the slot cut is centered on the mitered end of the workpiece and then plunge the end into the bit.

6 APPLY GLUE AND ASSEMBLE the top frame (Q, R) with biscuits.

7 CUT THE GLASS RETAINER STRIPS (S, T) to size. Finish the top frame and glass retainer strips before installing the glass and attaching the top to the case.

Make the base

1 MILL THE PARTS for the base (U, V). Rip them to width, but leave a few inches extra length for now.

2 USING A TABLESAW and dado set, cut a ¼" rabbet ⅜" deep where shown in **Figure 1**.

3 TABLE-ROUT the ¼" radius cove on the outside top edges.

4 CUT THE BASE PIECES to fit the box. To do this, miter one end of the two side pieces (V), clamp them to the box, and then mark and miter the front and rear pieces (U) to fit. Next, clamp the finished pieces to the front and back of the box and trim the sides to fit.

5 CHUCK A 1 ⅜" DIAMETER FORSTNER BIT in your drill press to cut the coves for the foot profile. Remove the remainder of the waste using a bandsaw.

6 APPLY GLUE TO THE RABBETS and miters and attach the parts to the bottom of the case. Once the glue dries, make and install the glue blocks (W) where shown in **Figure 1** to reinforce the miters.

Make the drawers

1 CUT THE DRAWER FRONTS and backs (X) and sides (Y) to a hair undersize to fit the opening. Cut the bottoms (Z) to size from ¼" thick plywood (see **Figure 2**).

2 **REFERRING TO Figure 2**, use a tablesaw and dado head to cut the ¼" rabbets ¼" deep along the ends of the drawer fronts and backs (X) and their mating dadoes on the inside faces of the sides (Y) to create the lock rabbet joints. Then cut the grooves along the inside faces of the fronts, backs, and sides for the drawer bottoms (Z).

3 Drill the ⅜" diameter counterbores ¼" deep and the ³⁄₁₆" diameter through-holes in the drawer fronts (X) where shown in **Figure 2**. (The oversized through-holes will allow drawer adjustment later.)

4 Glue up the drawers. Use a hand plane or sanding block to trim the drawers' sides and edges to create a snug, easy fit.

Install a full mortise lock set

1 Cut the false fronts (AA) a hair undersize. Drill holes for the pulls. Referring to **Figure 2**, lay out the central locations of the lock sets on the top edges.

2 Using a drill press equipped with a ⁷⁄₁₆" Forstner bit, adjust the depth and drill shallow mortises

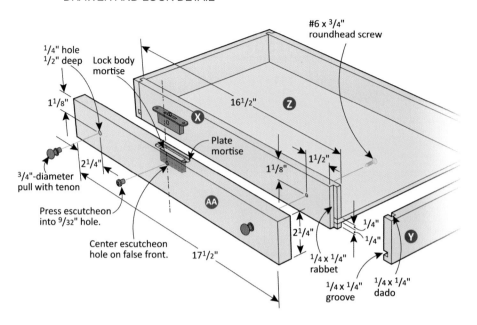

Fig. 2
DRAWER AND LOCK DETAIL

matching the lock plate lengths as shown in **Photo H**. Straighten the outer edges with a chisel.

3 Chuck a ¼" brad-point bit in the drill press and hog out the ⅝" deep mortises (or as needed) for the lock bodies. Pare the walls of the mortises flat as shown in **Photo I**.

4 Measure the distance from the top of the lock to the key pin and mark the location on the false fronts (AA). Lay

out the location of the escutcheons and drill the ⁹⁄₃₂" diameter hole **(Photo J)**, but don't install the escutcheons yet.

6 Test the fit of the lock. Then drill pilot holes for the screws and install the locks.

7 Attach the false drawer fronts (AA) to the drawer boxes with #6 × ¾" roundhead wood screws. Install the drawers, adjust the false fronts as necessary to even out the gaps, and then tighten down the screws.

Drill the mortise for the lock plate, then drill the lock body mortise without changing the fence setting.

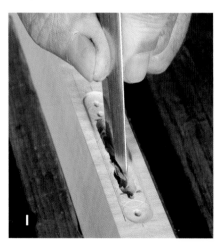

Focus on keeping the chisel vertical when paring the scalloped walls and rounded ends.

A cherry backer serves as an easy-to-read depth gauge. Stop as soon as you see darker sawdust.

Dividing Drawers

Egg crate dividers are simple to make and easy to remove or replace, but to look good, the lap joints must be cut precisely. I made this simple jig using a piece of plywood and divider stock scraps. The dimensions given here will create 15 openings, each 2.95 (2 $\frac{61}{64}$ ") × 2¾", but I've provided a formula so that you can adapt the jig to create different evenly-sized compartments. (For the jig to work, your divider stock must be consistent. Thickness, rip, and crosscut your divider stock (BB, CC) carefully to ensure that the parts are identical.)

Make the jig as shown. Mark stop-to-notch distances on it, and then clamp it to your miter gauge. Adjust the dado width to match the divider thickness, set the height a hair above half the width, and make a through-cut on the fence. Unclamp the fence, flip it end for end, and make a second through-cut.

To use the jig, butt a pair of long drawer dividers (BB) against the inside of the stop as shown and cut the first notch. Then lift the pair, fit them over the stop, and make your second cut. Now rotate the pair and repeat.

To notch the short dividers (CC), rotate the fence, set the stock against the stop, and cut the notch. Rotate the stock and cut the second notch.

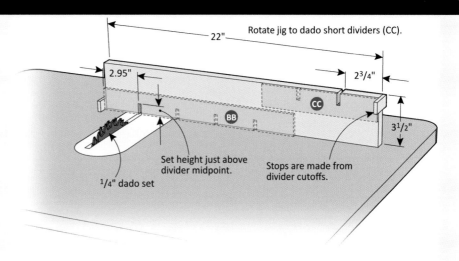

Rotate jig to dado short dividers (CC).

22"

2.95"

2¾"

CC

BB

3½"

Set height just above divider midpoint.

¼" dado set

Stops are made from divider cutoffs.

Notch spacing = (Drawer opening - divider thicknesses) / # of compartments. Long Dividers (25¾" - 1") / 5 = 2.95 (2 $\frac{61}{64}$ ")
Short Dividers (8¾" - 1/2")/3 = 2¾"

Finishing up

1 Sand the box through 220 grit. Dye the drawer fronts to match the side panels and then brush several coats of 1½-pound cut garnet shellac on all exterior surfaces.

2 Install the glass in the top frame assembly (Q, R). To do this, I tacked the glass retaining strips to the top frame with a 23-gauge pin nailer.

3 Attach the top frame assembly to the box with an offset screwdriver and (8) #4 × ¾" flathead wood screws. Install the knobs and press-fit the escutcheons.

4 Now dress up the drawer interiors as shown in "Lining Drawers with Fabric" on page 33.

5 Build dividers ("Dividing Drawers" shown above), insert them, and add your collection. 🪚

Convenience-*PLUS* BUYING GUIDE

	ITEM
☐ 1.	Quilted Maple Veneer Pack, 3 sq. ft.
☐ 2.	Titebond Cold Press Veneer Glue, 1 qt.
☐ 3.	TransTint Dye, Honey Amber, 2 oz.
☐ 4.	Freud Adjustable Tenon 2-Piece Rail and Stile Bit Set, Round Profile, (½" SH)
☐ 5.	Whiteside Cove Bit, ¼" R, ½" CL (½" SH)
☐ 6.	WoodRiver ⅛" Slot Cutter
☐ 7.	WoodRiver ½" SH Arbor w/Bearing (for use with slot cutter)
☐ 8.	Full Mortise Small Box Locks (4 needed)
☐ 9.	Liberon Garnet Shellac Flakes
☐ 10.	WoodRiver 1⅜" Forstner Bit
☐ 11.	Clear Tempered Glass, ⅛ × 9³/₁₆ × 16³/₁₆", Available At Local Glass Shops
☐ 12.	Mini-biscuits, 1⅛", #05J31.01, $11.80 (pkg. of 100); Smooth Knobs, ¾ × ¾" #02G14.15, $1.10 each, (8 needed), Available From Lee Valley, (800) 871-8158 or *leevalley.com*
☐ 13.	Loden-green Baize, $50/yard (1 yard needed). Available from Londonderry Brasses, (610) 593-6239 or *londonderry-brasses.com*
☐ 14.	Bainbridge Board, Three 20 × 30" Sheets, Available At Arts And Crafts Stores

Collector's Box Cut List

		Thickness	Width	Length	Qty.	Mat'l
A*	Side panels	¼"	7¾"	7¾"	2	VPly
B*	Back panel	¼"	7¾"	14¾"	1	VPly
C	Side upper rail	¾"	2¼"	7³/₁₆"	2	C
D	Side lower rail	¾"	2½"	7³/₁₆"	2	C
E	Side stiles	¾"	2¼"	11¾"	4	C
F	Back upper rail	¾"	2¼"	14³/₁₆"	1	C
G	Back lower rail	¾"	2½"	14³/₁₆"	1	C
H	Back stiles	¾"	2"	11¾"	2	C
I	Upper drawer dividers	½"	1¼"	17½"	1	C
J	Lower drawer divider	¾"	1⅜"	17½"	1	C
K	Upper drawer runners	½"	1"	9½"	6	M
L	Lower drawer runners	¾"	1"	8¾"	2	M
M	Upper drawer kickers	½"	¾"	9"	2	C
N	Rear screw cleat	½"	½"	17½"	1	M
O	Lower drawer support	¾"	⅝"	17½"	1	M
P	Drawer guides	⁷/₃₂"	½"	7"	4	M
Q*	Top frame (front/rear)	⅝"	1⅞"	19¼"	2	C
R*	Top frame (sides)	⅝"	1⅞"	12¼"	2	C
S	Glass retainer strips (front/rear)	³/₁₆"	¼"	16"	2	C
T	Glass retainer strips (side)	³/₁₆"	¼"	8¾"	2	C
U*	Base (front/rear)	¾"	1¾"	19¼"	2	C
V*	Base (side)	¾"	1¾"	12¼"	2	C
W	Glue blocks	¾"	¾"	1½"	4	C
X**	Drawer front/back	½"	2¼"	16½"	8	M
Y**	Drawer sides	½"	2¼"	10"	8	M
Z	Drawer bottoms	¼"	9½"	16½"	4	Ply
AA**	Drawer false fronts	¾"	2¼"	17½"	4	M
BB	Drawer dividers (long)	¼"	1¾"	15¾"	8	C
CC	Drawer dividers (short)	¼"	1¾"	8¾"	16	C

*Indicates parts that are initially cut oversized. See instructions.
** Indicates parts that are undersized by ¹/₃₂"

Materials: VPly=Maple Veneered over Baltic Birch Plywood, C=Cherry; M=Maple, Ply=Baltic Birch Plywood

Supplies: (8) #4 × ¾" flathead wood screws for attaching top, (8) #6 × ¾" roundhead wood screws for attaching the false fronts.

LINING DRAWERS WITH FABRIC

Finish interiors faster. Cut, stick, and fit.

By Craig Bentzley

Unless you're an aspiring pirate, it's unlikely that you'd take the time to build a finely crafted box and then dump in the contents. To display and protect treasures stored within, drawers and boxes deserve interiors that are finished as nicely as the exteriors. I've tried many drawer-lining methods, but I think fabric is the simplest and most practical solution. It's fast to use, flexible, and especially well-suited for last-minute gifts. As soon as the glue dries, you can press the project into service. Another

plus to liners is the flexibility afforded by the fabric. By picking a different material, you can easily customize an interior for anything from silverware to your best set of chisels.

Having lined hundreds of drawers over the past 35 years, I know that the process can be quick and easy or a messy disaster. To avoid the latter, I developed a simple three-step procedure that ensures smooth, snug-fitting liners. Once you've mastered the basics, you can employ the same approach on all types of compartments.

Neatness Counts

There's no magic in lining a drawer, but keeping the finished liners free of glue and smudges can present a challenge. Try these tricks:

• Cover your bench with craft paper. Recycling newspaper is fine in theory, but it can leave ink smudges on your finished liners.

• Use a fresh sheet of paper between every batch of liners.

• Clean your fingers (I use acetone) as soon as they feel sticky, before the excess glue finds its way onto the fabric.

• Go gloveless. If you can feel any excess glue, you're less likely to wipe it off where it's not wanted.

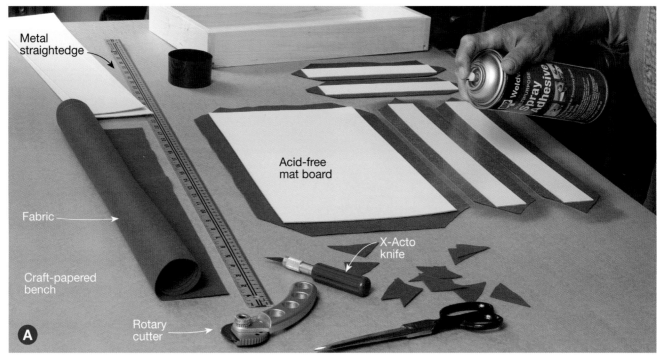

Labels on image:
- Metal straightedge
- Acid-free mat board
- X-Acto knife
- Fabric
- Craft-papered bench
- Rotary cutter
- A

Spray a thin coat of adhesive on the exposed liner and backer's outer edges. Use craft paper to maintain a stick-free work surface.

Stocking up

WHILE WOODWORKERS SHY AWAY from craft and fabric stores, I consider these some of the best sources for liner materials, tools, and other items that make the job easier and the end result last longer. For example, I've found that a rotary cutter, the same tool used by quilters, is perfect for slicing liner fabrics. Instead of making backers from scrap cardboard, I use mat board (sold as Bainbridge board); it's stiff, easy to wrap, and acid-free, which eliminates problems associated with cheaper materials, including discolored fabric and tarnished valuables.

If you plan to do a lot of lining, buy a self-healing cutting mat. This will protect your workbench top from damage and extend the life of cutting edges.

Lining in three steps

1 CUT THE PARTS TO FIT.

2 CUT THE BACKER FIRST. Measure the interior and then cut the mat board slightly undersized to allow for the thickness of the fabric. The actual allowance depends on the material you're using. I measure the liner's thickness with calipers and subtract twice that amount from the mat board's length and width. (If you have extra material, you can also make a test liner.) Cut the mat board using a straightedge and X-Acto knife.

3 SIZE THE LINER material about 2" larger than the backer and cut it with a rotary cutter. To make the fabric easier to fold, trim the corners at a 45° angle with a pair of scissors, staying about ⅛" away from the corners of the mat board.

Spray, stick, and fold

YOU'RE NOW READY TO AFFIX THE LINER to the backer. For larger-size projects, apply a thin coat of white glue to the fabric-side face of the mat board before laying it on the fabric. This prevents the fabric from creeping and drooping. For small- to medium-size compartments, like the drawers for the collector's box, simply place the liner face down and center the mat board backer on top.

SPRAY A LIGHT COAT OF ADHESIVE on the edges of the mat board and the fabric, as shown in **Photo A**. Because working times vary from five minutes to two hours, read the can and follow the instructions for a permanent bond.

WHEN THE ADHESIVE IS READY, work your way around each panel, folding and pressing the fabric down as you go, as shown in **Photo B**. Trim any overlapping fabric at the corners with an X-Acto knife, as shown in **Photo C**.

Glue and clamp

TIP ALERT Smooth out the liner before attaching it. Lay it out the night before to let any wrinkles relax. Then iron out any stubborn ones.

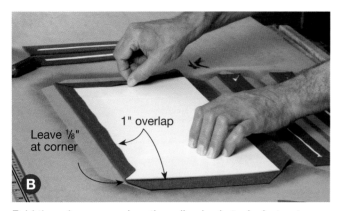

Leave ⅛"
at corner

1" overlap

B

Fold the edges over when the adhesive is tacky but not fully dry. Focus on clean folds and clean fingers.

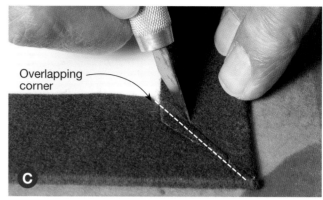

Overlapping corner

C

Cut through and remove the excess liner so the finished panel lies flat.

TO ATTACH THE LINED PANELS to the compartment, apply glue to the perimeter of each panel and clamp it in place. After installing the bottom, attach the sides. I prefer to install them in opposing pairs rather than in contiguous order. That way, I can clamp each with a full-length caul for complete pressure, leaving no residual indentations in the fabric. I typically install the left and right sides first, letting the glue dry before installing the front and back **(Photo D)**. 🪵

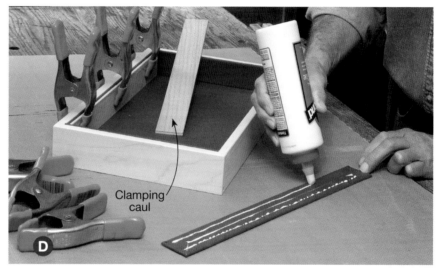

Clamping caul

D

Run a few beads of yellow or white glue to stick the lined panels to the interior. Use clamps and cauls to hold in place until the glue dries.

Liner Options

With liner materials, you get what you pay for. The good stuff looks better, lasts longer, and is easier to install. A yard of material can line a lot of drawers.

Felt ($8/yd., 72" wide roll) Cheap and readily available, but it fades quickly and doesn't wear well. OK, in a pinch.

Baize ($45/yd., 65" wide roll) This woven-wool fabric is similar to what you'd find lining a pool table.

Silverware cloth ($23/yd., 58" wide roll) A heavy cotton flannel specially treated to protect silverware and jewelry from tarnishing.

Ultra Suede ($45/yd., 45" wide roll) A synthetic fabric

that's soft as suede, but is stain-resistant and washable.

Velour ($25/yd., 58" wide roll) A nice way to finish small jewelry boxes. For best results, use a cotton non-stretch variety.

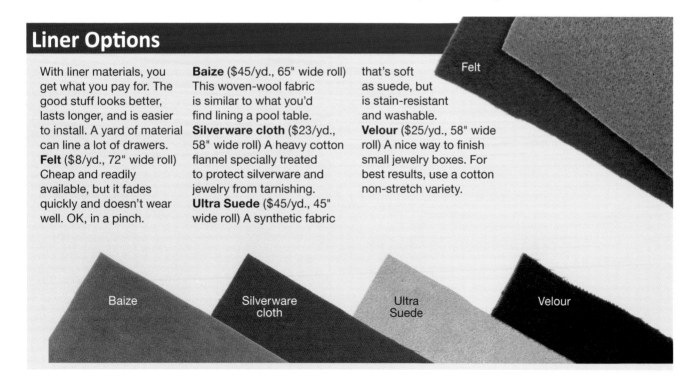

Felt

Baize

Silverware cloth

Ultra Suede

Velour

PAGODA-STYLE JEWELRY BOX

Discover an intriguing way to hang drawers.

By Bob Dickey

Overall dimensions: 14"w × 9½"d × 8¾"h

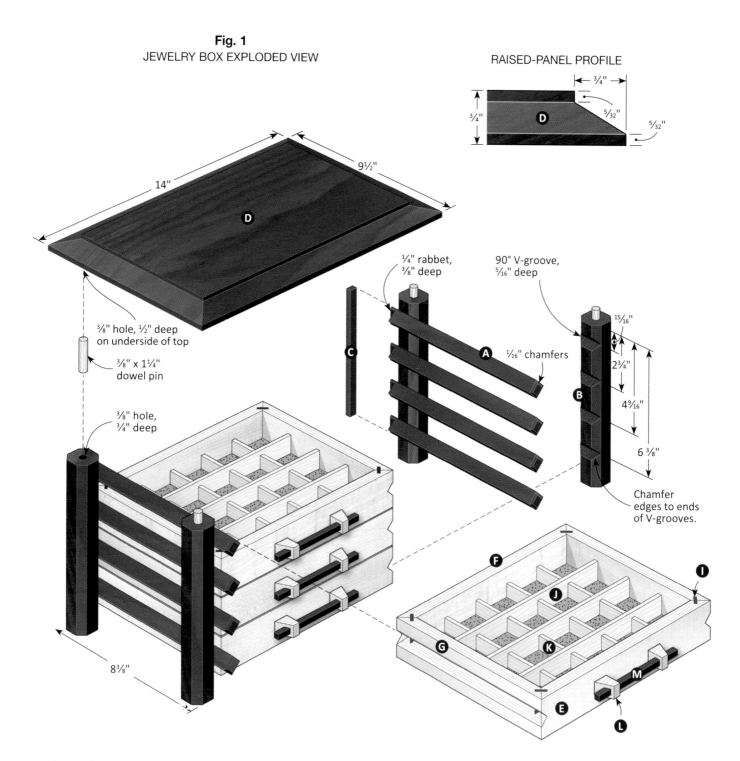

Fig. 1
JEWELRY BOX EXPLODED VIEW

RAISED-PANEL PROFILE

3/4"

3/4"

5/32"

D

5/32"

14"

9½"

D

¼" rabbet, 3/8" deep

90° V-groove, 5/16" deep

3/8" hole, ½" deep on underside of top

3/8" x 1¼" dowel pin

C

A

1/16" chamfers

15/16"

2¾"

B

4 9/16"

3/8" hole, 3/4" deep

6 3/8"

Chamfer edges to ends of V-grooves.

8 3/8"

F

I

J

G

K

M

E

L

This Asian-influenced box, with its broad beveled top and pagoda styling, features a drawer-hanging system that doubles as a dominant design element. Contrasting woods contribute to the overall look, as do the custom-made pulls. Splines join the mitered drawer corners, while the V-grooves cut in the drawer sides provide purchase on the wooden slides attached to the legs.

Precision setup and machining are key in the construction, made possible by a collection of simply-made jigs. I'll walk you through a successful building experience, so that, in the end, you'll have a worthy holiday gift item and a bucketful of new skills guaranteed to pay forward on later projects.

A

Align the point of the V-groove bit with the appropriate line on the setup jig to accurately adjust the fence. Lock the fence in place.

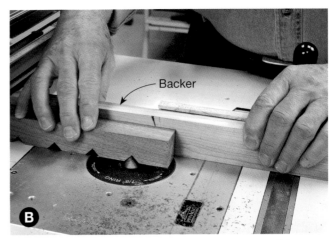

B

Start at the top ends and cut the top V-grooves in all four legs at one location before moving to the next V-groove set. Back the cuts to prevent tear-out.

Fig. 2
V-GROOVE SPACING JIG

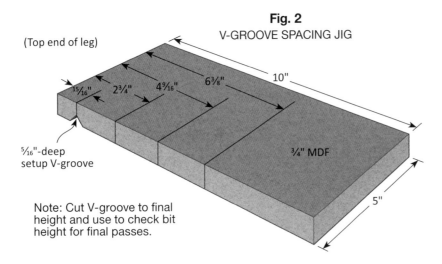

(Top end of leg)

$^{15}/_{16}$" 2^3/$_4$" 4^9/$_{16}$" 6^3/$_8$" 10"

^{5}/$_{16}$"-deep setup V-groove

^{3}/$_4$" MDF

5"

Note: Cut V-groove to final height and use to check bit height for final passes.

Build the open sides

1 RIP TWO 48" LONG WALNUT STRIPS to $^{11}/_{16}$" square and then surface them to ^{5}/$_8$" square. Crosscut the strips into eight 9" long pieces for the drawer slides (A) shown in **Figure 1**.

2 CHUCK A CHAMFERING BIT into a table-mounted router and, using a miter gauge or pushblock, cut ^{1}/$_{16}$" chamfers at the front ends of the slides (A).

3 RIP A 40" LENGTH of 6/4 (1^1/$_2$" thick) walnut stock to 1^5/$_{16}$" square. Now, surface the piece to 1^1/$_4$" square. Set up a stop on a tablesaw or mitersaw and cut four jewelry box legs (B) to the **Cut List** (page 45) length.

4 LAY OUT THE V-GROOVES precisely where shown in **Figure 2** on MDF or scrap plywood for a setup jig.

5 NEXT, INSTALL a 90° V-groove bit in your table-mounted router. Using the setup jig, adjust the fence, as shown in **Photo A**. Routing in increments, cut a ^{5}/$_{16}$" V-groove in the jig where shown in **Figure 2**. Use it to establish the needed bit height for the final pass for each leg V-groove.

6 CUT THE V-GROOVES across one face of each leg (B). Rout the top groove in all four legs first before moving to the next set of four V-grooves. Adjust the fence for each set, making three or more passes per set until the V-grooves

measure ^{5}/$_{16}$" deep. When making the cuts, back the workpieces with a miter-gauge extension fence or wood block, as shown in **Photo B,** to prevent tear-out. Before taking down the setup, lay the slides (A) in the grooves for two legs that make up one side. Place a straightedge across the slides to verify that they lay flat and are at the same height. Tweak any nonconforming cut.

7 USE THE SAME BIT to chamfer all four corners of the legs (B), where shown in **Figure 1**. With the bit raised to full height, cut the chamfers in increments, adjusting the fence as needed. Stop cutting when the edges of the chamfers intersect the point of the V-grooves. Sand the flat surfaces of the legs to 150 grit.

8 REFERRING TO Figure 3, make the **Side Glue-Up Jig** and two 6" wide spacers from scrap.

9 SET THE LEGS (B) for the left and right side assemblies in the jig, spacing them 6" apart with the spacers. Apply glue in the V-grooves for one side assembly, and set the slides (A) in the grooves. Ensure that the innermost leg and back ends of the slides are flush by snugging them against the jig's center rail. Also make sure the front leg is snug to the spacer. Use a clamped or weighted caul to

Fig. 3
SIDE GLUE-UP JIG WITH SPACER

MDF spacer
(make two)

6"
6"

#8 × 2"
screw

¾" × 1½" × 18"
maple

¾" × 1½" × 12½"
maple

L

8⅝"

¾" melamine

R

18"

13¼"

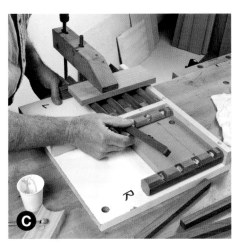

Use a simple jig and spacers to build box sides that mirror each other.

TIP ALERT

To keep the slides and stops from slipping during glue-up, tack them in place with 23-gauge pins.

press the slides firmly and evenly into the grooves. Repeat for the remaining side, as shown in **Photo C.** Remove any squeeze-out around the slides.

10 ATTACH A SACRIFICIAL FENCE to the tablesaw fence and install a ¼" dado set. Raise the blade to ⅜".

Now, referring to **Figure 1**, cut the rabbets on the back ends of the slides by running the side assemblies (A, B) along the fence.

11 FROM ¼" STOCK, rip a ⅜" wide piece long enough for the two drawer stops (C). Crosscut the pieces to finished length, test their fit in the slide rabbets, and then glue and clamp the stops in place.

Add the top to the sides

1 FROM 4/4 (1" THICK) WALNUT stock, glue up a blank to make the finished top (D). Trim the piece to the size in the **Cut List**. (If you have a piece wide enough, go with that.) Now, plane the blank to ¾" thick and finish-sand, ensuring flat surfaces.

2 CHUCK A BEVEL-PROFILE, raised-panel bit in a table-mounted router. As shown in the **Raised-Panel Profile** in

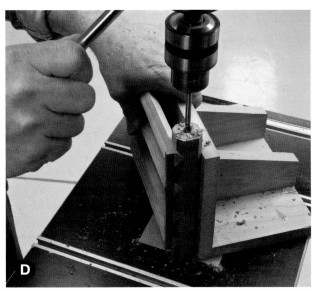

Use a right-angle fence to drill perfectly vertical holes into the leg ends for ⅜" diameter dowels.

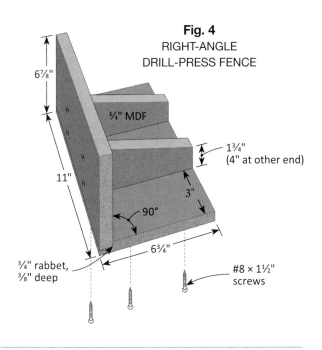

Fig. 4
RIGHT-ANGLE DRILL-PRESS FENCE

6⅞"

¾" MDF

1¾"
(4" at other end)

11"

3"

90°

6¾"

¾" rabbet,
⅜" deep

#8 × 1½"
screws

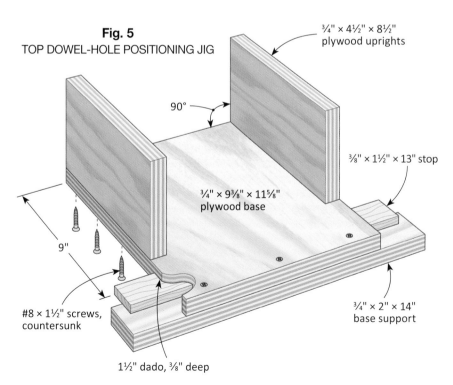

⅜" dowel center

E

Use the positioning jig in combination with dowel centers to accurately locate the dowel holes on the underside of the top.

Figure 1, you'll want the final cut to result in vertical edges bordering the tapered section to be equal in width. Shape the top (D) in steps, profiling the cross-grain ends first and the long-grain edges second to minimize tear-out. Sand the surfaces to 180 grit.

3 CONSTRUCT THE RIGHT-ANGLE DRILL-PRESS FENCE in Figure 4.

4 MARK THE CENTER on the top of each leg (B), and then chuck a ⅜" Forstner bit in your drill press. Holding a side assembly to the drill-press fence, drill a centered ¾" deep hole in each leg, as shown in **Photo D**. Do the other side assembly, too.

5 BUILD THE DOWEL-HOLE POSITIONING JIG in Figure 5 from

scrap. When in use, this spacing jig ensures that the distance between the side assemblies (A, B, C) is the same at the front and back and that the assemblies stand vertically.

6 INSERT ⅜" DOWEL CENTERS in the leg holes, and place the side assemblies against the positioning jig, as shown in **Photo E**. Center the top (D) on the leg assemblies, and press down to mark for the locations for the mating dowel holes (see **Figure 1** for reference).

7 WITH THE ⅜" FORSTNER BIT, drill ½" deep holes in the underside of the top (D) at the marks.

8 TRIM ⅜" DOWELS to just under 1¼" long. Now insert them in the leg holes, and dry-fit the top (D) onto the legs (B) to make sure the dowels seat fully. Now, apply glue to each hole and dowel, and attach the side assemblies (A, B, C) to the top (D). Check the alignment with a square, and adjust the side assemblies vertically if needed.

Machine the drawer parts

1 REFERRING TO THE CUT LIST, prepare enough stock for the drawers by surfacing a maple board to ⁹⁄₁₆" thick. (Because I used tiger maple for the fronts, I actually surfaced two separate boards to that thickness.) Now rip the stock to 1⅞" wide. Cut the fronts (E), backs (F), and sides (G) ½" longer than their final lengths.

2 SET UP THE TABLESAW for a 45° miter cut, and then miter one end of each drawer piece (E, F, G), removing about ¼" in the process. Now, using a stop, cut the drawer fronts (E) and backs (F) to 10" **(Photo F)**. Adjust the stop and cut the sides (G) to 8".

3 BUILD THE SPLINE SLOTTING JIG in Figure 6 to hold the drawer fronts (E), backs (F), and sides (G) at

Fig. 5
TOP DOWEL-HOLE POSITIONING JIG

¾" × 4½" × 8½" plywood uprights

90°

⅜" × 1½" × 13" stop

¾" × 9⅜" × 11⅝" plywood base

¾" × 2" × 14" base support

9"

#8 × 1½" screws, countersunk

1½" dado, ⅜" deep

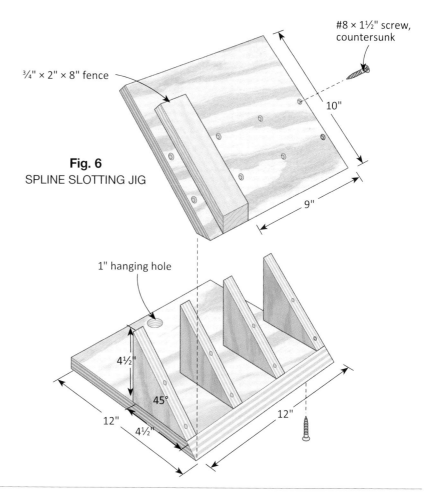

F Miter-cut the drawer fronts, backs, and sides to final length with a miter-gauge fence and accurately placed stopblock.

G With the slot-cutting bit installed (inset), hold the mitered workpiece snug to the jig's fence and make the cut.

a 45° angle to the router table while cutting spline slots perpendicular to the mitered ends.

4 INSTALL A ⁵⁄₃₂" SLOT-CUTTING BIT in the router table. Now, adjust the bit height to cut a slot in the mitered ends of drawer parts (E, F, G) ⅛" in from the inside faces. Adjust the fence to cut ¼" deep into the wood, and slot-cut the parts **(Photo G)**.

5 RIP THE DRAWER FRONTS (E), backs (F), and sides (G) to final width, removing any edges with tear-out if needed.

6 ADJUST THE SAW BLADE to ³⁄₁₆" high, and move the fence ⁵⁄₃₂" from it. Now, make the first groove cuts for the drawer bottoms (H) on the inside faces of the drawer fronts (E), backs (F), and sides (G) (see **Figure 7**). Using the plywood for the bottom as a gauge (I used ⁵⁄₃₂" thick material), adjust the fence and make a second cut in one piece and test the fit. If satisfied, enlarge the grooves on the other parts.

7 LAY A RULER IN THE DRAWER bottom grooves cut in step 6 to measure the length and width required for the bottoms (H). Measure the bottom groove length of one front (E) or back (F) and a side (G).

8 CUT THE BOTTOMS (H) to size and test-fit. The bottoms can be ¹⁄₃₂" shorter all around with no problem.

9 FINALLY, MEASURE THE LENGTH of the grooves on the drawer parts (E, F, G) to where they intersect

the spline slots. Then use a fine-tooth handsaw to nip off the corners of the bottoms (H) to those dimensions to provide thorough clearance for the splines. (I usually cut off about ³⁄₁₆" from each corner, but measure first to verify.)

Fig. 6
SPLINE SLOTTING JIG

#8 × 1½" screw, countersunk

¾" × 2" × 8" fence

10"

9"

1" hanging hole

4½"

45°

12"

4½"

12"

41

With the drawer parts held snugly together using a band clamp, apply glue to the splines and tap them into corner slots.

Cut the splines and assemble the drawers

1 USING A CARRIER BOARD, plane a piece of 2" wide walnut stock to a hair over $\frac{5}{32}$" thick for the splines (I). Test-fit an edge of the piece in a spline slot. Sand the piece, if needed. (I used a drum sander to sneak up on the fit, but a simple handheld block sander would suffice.) You want a sliding fit in the slots with no slop.

2 NEXT, DETERMINE THE WIDTH of your spline stock by first clamping the parts of one drawer (E, F, G, H) together. Now, measure the total width of the two adjacent spline slots at one corner. (Ideally, it should be exactly $\frac{1}{2}$".) Set up a stand-off on your tablesaw fence, and trim one cross-grain spline (I) to the width determined. Test-fit the piece in the assembled drawer. Adjust the width if needed, and cut the remaining splines (you need a total of 16). Consider dry-fitting the other drawers and test-fitting all of the splines for a precision fit.

3 SAND THE INSIDE FACES of the drawer fronts (E), backs (F), sides (G), and both faces of the bottom (H) to 150 grit.

4 DRY-FIT THE DRAWER PARTS for one drawer (E, F, G, H), inserting the splines (I) and clamping the assembly with a band clamp. Check it for square and gapped joints. Make any needed corrections. Now, disassemble and apply glue to the spline slots and the mitered surfaces. Reassemble the drawer, pulling the parts together with the band clamp.

5 APPLY A LIGHT COAT OF GLUE to the splines and tap them into the corner joints, as shown in **Photo H**, making sure they bottom out. Check that the drawer is still square, and tighten the clamp. Remove any squeeze-out. Once the glue dries, remove the clamp and then cut and sand the splines flush with the box edges. Repeat for the remaining drawers.

Fig. 7
DRAWER VIEW EXPLODED

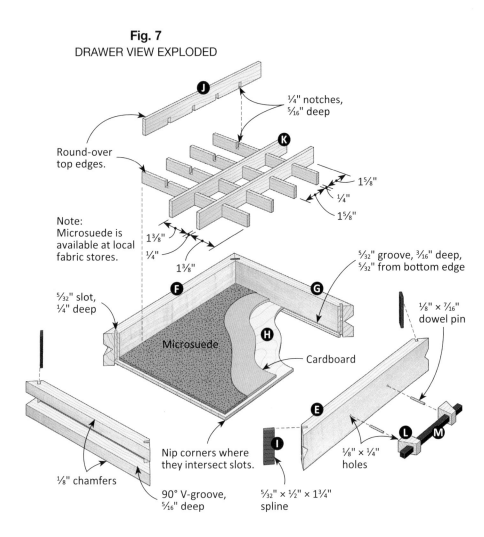

$\frac{1}{4}$" notches, $\frac{5}{16}$" deep

Round-over top edges.

Note: Microsuede is available at local fabric stores.

$1\frac{3}{8}$"
$\frac{1}{4}$"
$1\frac{3}{8}$"

$1\frac{5}{8}$"
$\frac{1}{4}$"
$1\frac{5}{8}$"

$\frac{5}{32}$" slot, $\frac{1}{4}$" deep

$\frac{5}{32}$" groove, $\frac{3}{16}$" deep, $\frac{5}{32}$" from bottom edge

$\frac{1}{8}$" × $\frac{7}{16}$" dowel pin

Microsuede

Cardboard

$\frac{1}{8}$" × $\frac{1}{4}$" holes

Nip corners where they intersect slots.

$\frac{1}{8}$" chamfers

90° V-groove, $\frac{5}{16}$" deep

$\frac{5}{32}$" × $\frac{1}{2}$" × $1\frac{3}{4}$" spline

Fit the drawers to the side assemblies

1 **MEASURE AND MARK** the exact center of the drawer sides (G). Now, install a horizontal V-groove bit in the router table, and adjust the fence so that the bit's point is dead center on the center mark.

2 **ADJUST THE ROUTER BIT** height to take an initial cut of around ³⁄₁₆" deep. Now, make an initial pass on both sides of the drawers, using a backer board to minimize chip-out. Make subsequent passes as shown in **Photo I**, increasing the depth each time and testing the fit of the drawer into the frame. The final groove should be about ⁵⁄₁₆" deep, but check each drawer's fit when making the final passes. This is where even minor variations in dimensions and tolerances come into play. The final fit should slide freely without slop. For the best fit, mark each drawer on its bottom outside face as to its intended location in the box.

3 **WITH THE DRAWERS** fitted, lower the router bit to cut a ¹⁄₈" chamfer along the top and bottom edges of all the drawer sides.

4 **FINAL-SAND** the drawers to 180 grit.

5 **MAKE THE TOP AND BOTTOM** egg-crate dividers (J, K), shown in **Figure 7**, for one or more drawers by first planing and ripping strips to the thickness and widths in the **Cut List**. Next, rout ¹⁄₈" round-overs on the top edges on each strip. Now, crosscut the needed number of pieces to length after confirming the dimension with the drawers. Bundle the top dividers into one group and the bottom dividers into another with double-faced tape, flushing the edges and ends. Lay out the ¹⁄₄" notches ⁵⁄₁₆" deep on the top piece of each bundle, where shown in the drawing, and cut them with a miter gauge and an extension fence outfitted with stops. Assemble the egg-crate dividers and test-fit them in the drawers.

Press the drawer box down and against the fence as you move it past the horizontal V-groove router bit (Inset).

Make the stylish pulls

1 **CUT A 20" LONG PIECE** of stock to ¹⁄₂" thick × ⁷⁄₈" wide for the pull supports (L). Mark across the width of the stock for correct reassembly after it has been ripped.

2 **REFERRING TO THE FIVE-STEP** sequence in **Figure 8**, raise your saw fence to ⁵⁄₈", rip a ¹⁄₈" piece off of the stock's width, and set the ¹⁄₈" piece aside.

3 **USING A FLAT TOOTH GRIND** (FTG) blade in your tablesaw, raise the height to ¹⁄₄" and make a test cut to achieve the exact dimension. Now, adjust the fence ¹⁄₈" from the blade. With the ripped edge of the narrow strip down, make the first of two adjacent groove cuts. Turn the piece end for end and make the second cut to create a ¹⁄₄" wide groove, ¹⁄₄" deep.

4 **APPLY A THIN LAYER OF GLUE** to the inside surface of the ¹⁄₈" thick strip. Align the strip with the marks on the grooved piece and then clamp it in place using spring clamps to hold it tight and flush. Remove any squeeze-out and let dry.

5 **SQUARE ONE END** of the blank and lay out the first pull support (L). Angle the miter gauge and extension fence at 25°, and clamp a stand-off to your saw's fence so that, after cutting the pull support, the wider end of the support measures

Working off the stand-off to establish the width of the finished pull support, hold the workpiece to the extension fence and make the 25° cut.

Fig. 8

PULL SUPPORTS IN 5 STEPS

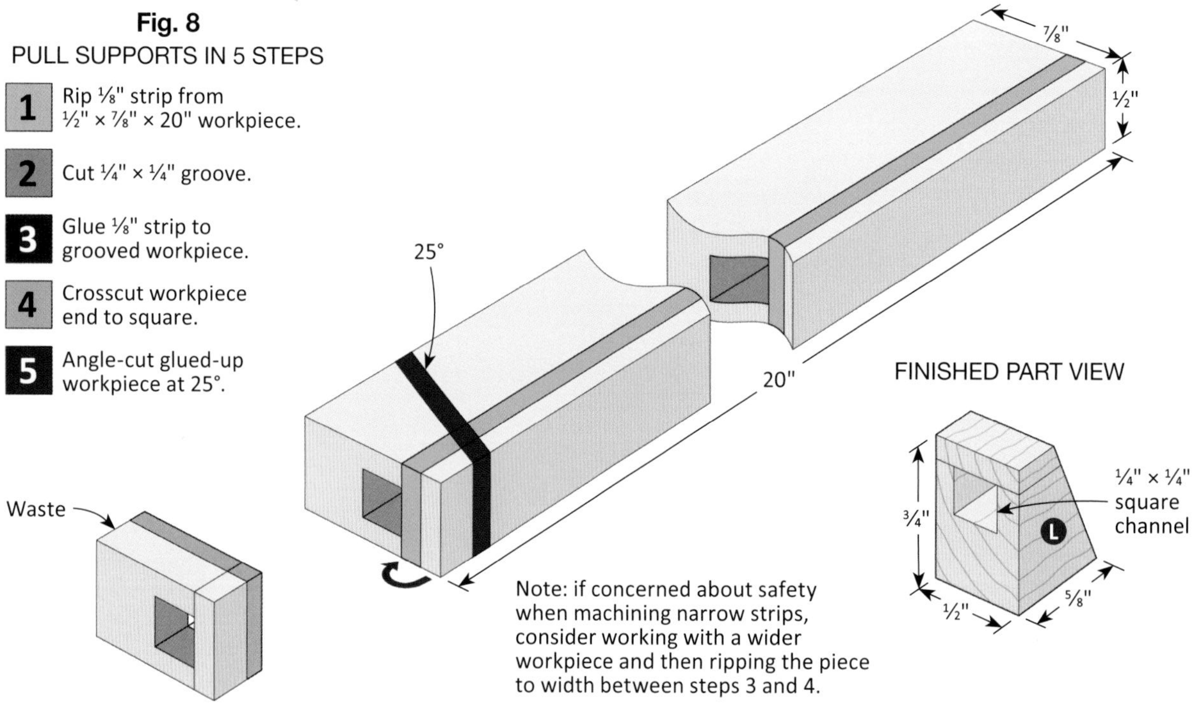

1 Rip ⅛" strip from ½" × ⅞" × 20" workpiece.

2 Cut ¼" × ¼" groove.

3 Glue ⅛" strip to grooved workpiece.

4 Crosscut workpiece end to square.

5 Angle-cut glued-up workpiece at 25°.

Waste

25°

20"

⅞"

½"

FINISHED PART VIEW

¼" × ¼" square channel

¾"

½"

⅝"

L

Note: if concerned about safety when machining narrow strips, consider working with a wider workpiece and then ripping the piece to width between steps 3 and 4.

⅝" wide. Now, position the stock against the miter gauge extension fence, making sure that the narrower side above the square hole touches the fence. Cut off a pull support. Square the workpiece before cutting the next pull support. (I alternate the miter gauge between the 90° and 25° settings.) Continue cutting **(Photo J)** until all eight pull supports are made. Sand the cut surfaces to remove chip-out and saw marks.

6 MEASURE THE WIDTH and depth of the square hole in a pull support (L) for the pull bars (M). Next, rip stock for these pieces to this exact dimension or slightly over, and sand for a good fit. Cut four pull bars to the **Cut List** length, and check that they slide through the holes.

7 CUT A 2½" WIDE SPACER block to align the pulls for glue-up. Now, position two pull supports (L) at opposite ends of the spacer block. Insert and center the pull bar (M) in the

square holes in the spacer blocks. Slide each pull support off slightly, place a drop or two of thin CA glue at the joint location, and reposition the supports. When the glue has set, lightly sand the assembly. Repeat for the remaining pull assemblies.

Attach the drawer pulls

1 STRIKE A CENTERLINE lengthwise on the drawer fronts (E). Next, draw lines corner to corner across the wide end of each pull support (L) to locate the centers.

2 SNIP THE HEADS off eight ¾" brads. Grasp the cut end of a brad in a drill chuck, and spin the brad into the pull support at a marked center. Do this for all the pull supports.

3 MARK ONE END OF EACH PULL assembly (L, M) as "left," and number each assembly 1-4. Similarly mark

the drawers. Now, carefully locate the brad points of one pull assembly on a corresponding drawer front (E), guiding on the centerline. Use spacers or an adjustable square to precisely center it between the drawer front ends and edges, and press the points into the wood **(Photo K)**. Do the same for the remaining assemblies.

4 PULL THE BRADS WITH PLIERS. Now, set up the drill press and, using a brad-point bit, drill ⅛" diameter holes ¼" deep in both the drawer fronts (E) and the pull supports (L).

5 CROSSCUT ⅛" DIAMETER DOWELS to ⁷⁄₁₆" long. Insert them in the pull assemblies (L, M) and test-fit them in the corresponding holes in drawer front (E). Check that they align drawer to drawer in the jewelry box. Now, remove the pull assemblies, add a drop or two of thin CA to the dowels, and press the assemblies in place.

6 **FINALLY, FINISH-SAND THE BOX,** and apply a clear finish of your choice (I used Deft Lacquer). Cut cardboard and drawer liner material to size. (I used metal-friendly Microsuede found at fabric stores, since it doesn't chemically react with jewelry). Fit them in place **(Figure 6)**. For more, see "Lining Drawers with Fabric" on page 33.

Using spacers to locate the pull assemblies, press the brads in the pull supports (inset) into the drawer fronts to mark them.

Pagoda-Style Box Cut List		Thickness	Width	Length	Qty.	Mat'l
A	Drawer slides	⁵/₈"	⁵/₈"	9"	8	W
B	Legs	1¼"	1¼"	8"	4	W
C	Drawer stops	¼"	³/₈"	6¼"	2	W
D*	Top	³/₄"	9½"	14"	1	W
E*	Drawer fronts	⁹/₁₆"	1³/₄"	10"	4	FM
F*	Drawer backs	⁹/₁₆"	1³/₄"	10"	4	M
G*	Drawer sides	⁹/₁₆"	1³/₄"	8"	8	M
H	Drawer bottoms	⁵/₃₂"	7³/₁₆"	9⁵/₁₆"	4	BP
I*	Splines	⁵/₃₂"	½"	1³/₄"	16	W
J	Top egg-crate dividers (left to right)	¼"	⁷/₈"	8¹³/₁₆"	6	M
K	Bottom egg-crate dividers (front to back)	¼"	⁵/₈"	6¹³/₁₆"	6	M
L*	Pull supports	½"	⁵/₈"	³/₄"	8	M
M	Pull bars	¼"	¼"	4⁵/₈"	4	W

*Parts initially cut oversized and then trimmed to fit. See instructions.
Materials: W = Walnut, FM = Figured Maple, M = Maple, BP= Birch Plywood
Hardware/Supplies: 1/8" dowels

CURVED-TOP VENEERED BOX

Simple elegance from a bent plywood panel

By Jonathan Benson

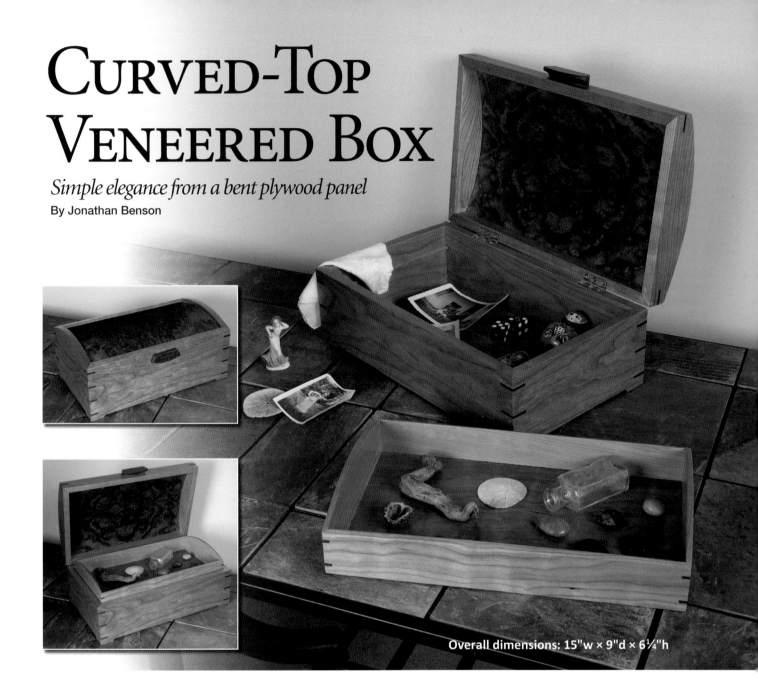

Overall dimensions: 15"w × 9"d × 6¼"h

When I design a project I often try to include a curve or two to add a touch of elegance. The curved top for this box is made with two pieces of ⅛" thick plywood sandwiched between two pieces of veneer and then bent in a simple shop-made form. The form is easy to build and is reusable for making multiples of this project. Although you could use two single continuous sheets of any type of veneer, I like to add another dimension to the design by creating a four-way matched pattern (see "Laying Up a Four-Way Match," page 56). The box itself is constructed using basic miter joints reinforced with contrasting splines **(Figure 1)**. Like many boxes, it's made by gluing up the walls with the top and bottom panels captured in their grooves, then sawing the lid free after assembly. I also added a decorative handle and a removable tray with curved sides that complement the shape of the box top.

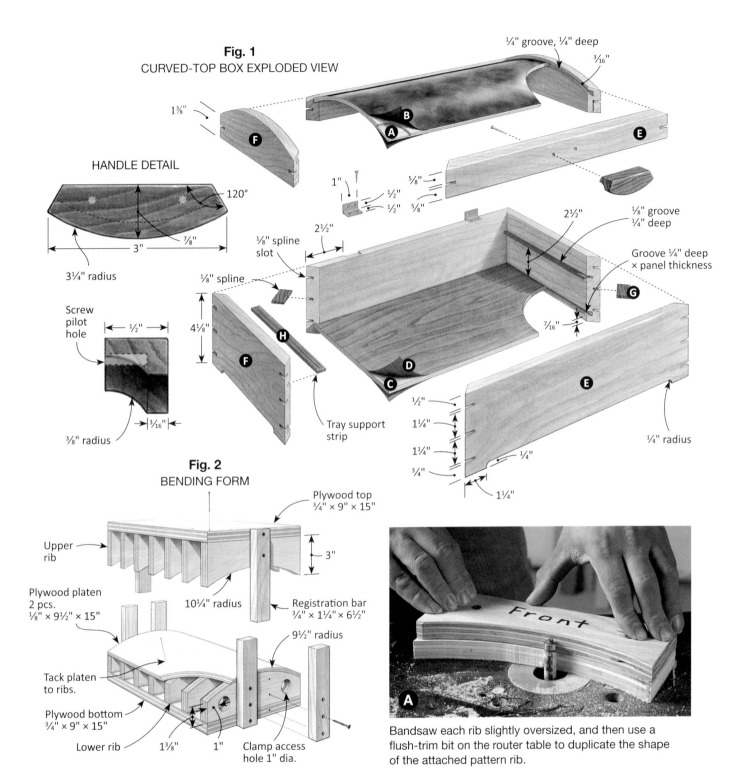

Fig. 1
CURVED-TOP BOX EXPLODED VIEW

¼" groove, ¼" deep

³/₁₆"

1³/₈"

F

B

A

E

HANDLE DETAIL

120°

3"

⅞"

3¼" radius

1"

½"

½"

⅝"

⅝"

2½"

⅛" spline slot

⅛" spline

2½"

⅛" groove ¼" deep

Groove ¼" deep × panel thickness

G

Screw pilot hole

½"

F

4⅛"

H

⁷/₁₆"

³/₈" radius

³/₁₆"

C

D

Tray support strip

E

½"

1¼"

1¼"

¾"

¼"

1¼"

¼" radius

Fig. 2
BENDING FORM

Plywood top ¾" × 9" × 15"

Upper rib

3"

Plywood platen 2 pcs. ⅛" × 9½" × 15"

10¼" radius

Registration bar ¾" × 1¼" × 6½"

Tack platen to ribs.

9½" radius

Plywood bottom ¾" × 9" × 15"

Lower rib

1³/₈"

1"

Clamp access hole 1" dia.

A

Front

Bandsaw each rib slightly oversized, and then use a flush-trim bit on the router table to duplicate the shape of the attached pattern rib.

First make the form

1 LAY OUT ONE UPPER and one lower rib **(Figure 2)** on ¾" thick plywood. Bandsaw the curves a bit shy of the cutline, and then carefully sand to the lines. *Note: The radii differ to account for the ¾" worth of platens and panels that will fit between the ribs during the panel glue-up.* You'll use these two "pattern" ribs for making the rest.

2 USE THE TWO PATTERN RIBS to mark out 12 additional ribs on ¾" thick plywood. Mark the same face of each piece for consistent orientation during assembly. To economize material, lay the ribs out in nesting fashion on a 9" wide panel. Then bandsaw each rib curve slightly oversized. Screw a pattern rib to each piece and trim the curve to final shape using a flush-trim bit on the router table **(Photo A)**.

Drill two 1" diameter clamp access holes in two of the bottom ribs where shown in **Figure 2**.

47

Use thick wooden cauls to distribute clamping pressure across the bending form.

Fig. 3
TOP PANEL GLUE-UP

Bending form rib

2-pc. upper platen (free-floating)

Paper

2-pc. box lid panel

2-pc. lower platen (tacked to jig)

3 BUILD THE BENDING FORM, nailing or screwing the ribs to the ¾" thick plywood panels, spaced evenly along the length of the form. Make sure that the marked faces of the ribs are all oriented in the same direction for consistency of curvature. Cut four pieces of ⅛" thick plywood to use as platens. Tack two of them to the bottom half of the form, but set the other two aside for use as top platens during glue-up later. (It's best not to attach them to the upper concave ribs.)

4 SCREW THE REGISTRATION BARS to the upper half of the form, squaring each one to the plywood top at the center. Align the two halves of the form and screw the registration bars to

the bottom section with veneer scrap separating them from the center bars for ease of operation.

Make the top and bottom box panels

1 TO MAKE THE TOP PANEL, begin by sawing two pieces of ⅛" thick plywood (A) to the rough size in the **Cut List** (page 51). Then cover one side of each with a sheet of veneer (B). Use the techniques described in "No-Fear Veneering" on page 52.

2 SAW THE BOTTOM PANEL (C) to rough size, making it from either two pieces of ⅛" thick plywood glued together or from a piece of ¼" thick

plywood. Apply veneer (D) to both sides of it, and then cut it to the finished size shown in the **Cut List**.

3 GLUE UP THE CURVED TOP using Titebond III, plastic resin glue, or other hard-drying adhesive. Spread the glue on the back of each panel using a small paint roller, and then place the panels back to back in the form on a piece of clean paper. Also lay a piece of paper over the top of the panels before

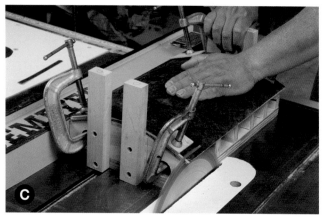

Shift the top panel on the bending form to align the cutline with the blade; then trim the edge.

Crosscut the top panel to finished width holding its concave side down on a crosscut sled.

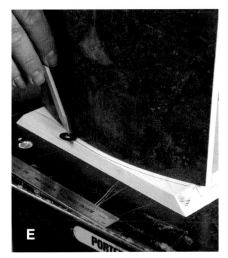

Mark out the curve on the end wall using a washer-guided pencil to offset the curve of the top panel.

Rout the top groove in each end wall using a curved fence that matches the curved edge of the wall.

covering them with the upper platens, as shown in **Figure 3**. Center the panels on the bottom platen, and put the top half of the form in place. Clamp the form together as shown in **Photo B**, and let it sit overnight.

4 MARK THE PANEL for ripping to final width. Gauge a line at each long edge of the panel that's parallel to the panel center (or the long veneer seam on a four-way match) and 4^7/$_{16}$" from it. Working on the tablesaw, clamp the panel to the bending form with one of the gauged lines aligned with the blade and parallel to its path. With the rip fence guiding the jig, make the cut as shown in **Photo C**. Then rotate the form and adjust the panel to make the opposite cut in the same manner.

5 MARK THE PANEL to finished length, measuring out 7^3/$_{16}$" from the center of the panel (or the short veneer seam). Saw to your lines using a crosscut sled **(Photo D)**.

Build the basic box

1 CUT THE WALLS of the box (E, F) to the sizes shown in the **Cut List**. If you cut all four walls from a single board and join them in sequence, the grain will flow continuously around three of the corners. (Orient the odd corner toward the back.)

2 MITER THE CORNERS, and then saw the ¼" deep grooves for the bottom panel where shown in **Figure 1**, gauging the width to fit snugly around the sanded panel. Also cut the grooves in the end walls for the tray support strips (H).

3 STAND THE TOP PANEL (A, B) on its end to lay out the curved groove on the inside face of one of the end walls (F). Locate the center of the panel a hair more than ³/₁₆" in from the top edge of the wall. Then equalize the distance between the panel corners and the top edge of the wall. Make a registration mark on the wall miter at each panel corner; then trace along both curved edges of the panel to lay out its groove on the wall. Finally, mark out the curved top edge of the box wall by guiding a pencil using a washer with a ³/₁₆" wide rim, as shown in **Photo E**.

4 BANDSAW SHY OF YOUR TOP EDGE layout line, and then carefully sand to it.

5 TRANSFER THE CURVE TO A BOARD that's long enough to span your router table. Saw out the curve and sand its edges to create a fence for routing the curved grooves in the end walls (F).

6 OUTFIT YOUR TABLE ROUTER with a ³/₁₆" diameter straight bit, and then clamp the fence in place ³/₁₆" from the bit. With the bit raised about ³/₁₆", rout the groove, feeding the box wall from right to left **(Photo F)**. Then groove the opposite end wall using the same setup. Raise the bit to ¼" and repeat the process. Reposition the fence about ¹/₁₆" further from the bit to rout the grooves to final width. Test the fit of the panel in both grooves. If necessary, readjust the fence away from the bit and take another shallow pass.

7 DRY-ASSEMBLE THE BOX with the bottom (C, D) in place. Mark out the top grooves on the front and back walls (E), carefully intersecting the ends of the curved grooves. Then use a bevel gauge to register the angle of the curved top edge in relation to the front or back wall. Tilt your tablesaw blade to this angle and rip the ¼" deep panel grooves in the front and back walls, resetting the rip fence as necessary to accommodate the thickness of the top. When you're done, leave the blade set at the angle.

8 SAND AND FINISH THE INSIDE faces of the walls, masking off the miter faces and tray support grooves before applying the finish. Also finish both faces of the top and bottom panels (see "Finishing Up" on page 55 for advice on finishing veneer).

Trim the excess at the top edges of the front and back walls with the blade set to the angle of the end wall.

Saw the spline slots using a runner-guided plywood cradle. A stopblock registers the cuts.

9 GLUE UP THE BOX with the top and bottom panels in place (do not glue the panels in their grooves). Make sure everything is square under clamp pressure with the box sitting on a dead-flat surface. Let the glue dry thoroughly.

10 WITH THE TABLESAW BLADE still set at its previous angle, adjust the rip fence to trim away the excess at the top edges of the front and back walls **(Photo G)**. Afterward, plane or sand as necessary to flush up and smooth the adjoining edges.

11 LAY OUT THE SPLINE SLOTS where shown in **Figure 1**. Cut them on the tablesaw, using a shop-made cradle to carry the box over the blade at a 45° angle to the table as shown in **Photo H**. Saw the slots as deep as possible without intersecting the box interior. Make splines (G) that fit snugly in the slots, glue them in place, and then saw and sand them flush to the walls.

Cut away the lid and hinge it in place

1 SEPARATE THE LID on the tablesaw by cutting through the front and both ends. Before sawing through the back, shim the previous cuts with ⅛" plywood to keep the parts from pinching the blade at the end of the cut. Use a band

clamp to hold everything in place, and then make the cut **(Photo I)**.

2 MAKE THE TRAY SUPPORT STRIPS (H), apply finish to their exposed edges, and then glue them into their grooves.

3 CUT THE HINGE MORTISES by laying each hinge in place on the box base with the axis of the hinge barrel aligned with the box edge. Now knife around the hinge perimeter. Rout out most of the waste; then pare to the knife lines with a chisel. Install each hinge with one screw. Clamp the lid on top of the folded hinges, and knick its edge at the ends of each hinge to mark the mortise locations. Then lay out and cut the lid mortises.

Shape the feet and make the handle

1 ROUT THE FOOT RECESSES using a router table outfitted with a ½" diameter spiral bit to minimize burning. Clamp a stopblock on either end of the fence, setting each to terminate the cut 1¼" from the ends of the box **(Photo J)**. Make a series of progressively deeper cuts to achieve a ¼" deep recess.

2 LAY OUT THE HANDLE on a ½" thick piece of stock about 4 × 8" **(Figure 1)**.

Locate the curve near the edge of the stock, extending its arc about ½" beyond each end of the handle. Bandsaw the arc, sand it smooth, and rout a ⅜" radius, ¼" deep, on the underside **(Photo K)**. Then saw out the rest of the shape and sand it. Set the finished handle aside for now.

Make the tray and finish up

1 REFERRING TO THE CUT LIST, saw the tray bottom (I) to rough size, glue veneer (J) to both sides, and then trim the bottom to its finished size.

2 MILL ¼" THICK STOCK for the tray's long sides (K) and ends (L). Referring to **Figure 4**, rip the long sides to width, bandsaw the tray ends, and

Make the final lid-separation cut after shimming and clamping the previous kerfs closed.

Rout the foot recesses using stopblocks to register the beginning and end of the cut.

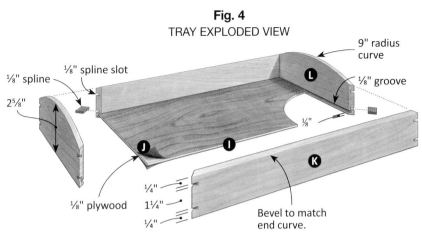

Fig. 4
TRAY EXPLODED VIEW

9" radius curve

⅛" spline slot

⅛" groove

⅛" spline

2⅝"

⅛"

⅛" plywood

¼"

1¼"

¼"

Bevel to match end curve.

J · I · K · L

sand the curves. Miter the corners and saw the ⅛" deep grooves to a width that accommodates the bottom panel (I, J).

3 SAND THE INTERIOR WALLS and bottom panel, glue the mitered corners, and clamp up the tray, making sure it's absolutely square. When the glue is dry, saw the spline slots, glue splines in place, and trim and sand them flush to the tray sides.

4 CHECK THE FIT of the tray inside the box. Then sand the tray, handle, and exterior walls of the box through 220 grit, and apply several coats of

finish to all. To attach the handle, clamp it in place, trace around it, remove it, and then mark the screw locations **(Figure 1)**. Drill screw clearance holes; then poke screws

through them into the handle to mark the pilot hole locations. Drill the pilot holes, and then screw the handle in place. Finish up by reinstalling the hinges. 🪵

Rout the handle cove on a large piece of stock before sawing out the full handle shape.

Curved-Top Box Cut List		Thickness	Width	Length	Qty.	Mat'l
Box and Lid						
A*	Top panel	⅛"	rough: 9½" finished: 8⅞"	rough 15" finished: 14⅜"	2	HP
B+	Top veneer		9½"	15"	2	WV
C*	Bottom panel	⅛"	rough: 8⅞" finished: 8⅜"	rough: 14⅞" finished: 14⅜"	2	HP
D+	Bottom veneer		8⅞"	14⅞"	2	CV
E	Front and back walls	⁹⁄₁₆"	6¾"	15"	2	C
F	End walls	⁹⁄₁₆"	6¾"	9"	2	C
G	Spline	⅛"	¾"	1½"	16	W
H	Tray support strips	⅛"	½"	7⅞"	2	C
Tray						
I*	Tray bottom	⅛"	rough: 7⅞" finished: 7½"	rough: 13⅞" finished: 13½"	1	HP
J+	Tray bottom veneer		7⅞"	13⅞"	2	CV
K	Tray long sides	¼"	2"	13¾"	2	C
L	Tray ends	¼"	2⅝"	7¾"	2	C

*Parts are initially cut oversized. Refer to story for additional instructions.
+Veneer is cut to match rough dimensions of substrate and then trimmed to size.
Materials: HP=Hardwood Plywood, WV=Walnut Veneer, CV=Cherry Veneer, C=Cherry, W=Walnut

No-Fear Veneering

Give your work a beautiful skin.

By Jonathan Benson

Veneering has been around since the age of the Pharaohs and has been used to create some of the finest furniture ever made. Applying a decorative "skin" of wood veneer to an underlying substrate can beautify mundane wood panels and stretch the use of rare, exotic, and expensive woods, many of which are difficult or impossible to find in lumber form these days. Another advantage is that, when properly glued to a sound substrate, veneer is very stable and not subject to seasonal expansion and contraction. Therefore, it can be arranged in any pattern or combination of species without danger of cracking or splitting. Many veneers are sliced in sequence from a log in closely matched sheets, allowing arrangement of many symmetrical or repeating patterns.

To the uninitiated, veneering can seem intimidating and complicated. But not to fear; I'll explain the basic tools and techniques that you need to get started. Then, as an exercise, I'll walk you through the steps for creating a "four-way" match, like the one used to make the box top on page 46 (see "Curved-Top Veneered Box").

A

Veneer offerings include many rare and figured species.

Choosing and storing veneer

VENEER IS AVAILABLE in a wide variety of species, figures, and sizes, in thicknesses ranging from $\frac{1}{20}$" to $\frac{1}{42}$" as shown in **Photo A**. The two common methods for producing veneer are rotary- and flitch-cutting. *Rotary-cut* veneer is made by pressing a long knife against a spinning log to peel away long, wide, continuous sheets, like those you commonly see on the faces of construction-grade plywood. *Flitch-cut* veneer is produced by knifing tangentially through the log in sequence, essentially slicing it into a stack of paper. This produces a series of closely matched sheets that you can arrange to create a variety of patterns like those shown in **Photo B** below. The bundle of sequentially matched veneers is called a *flitch*. I use flitch-cut veneers exclusively, as rotary-cutting doesn't offer the same design possibilities.

AS YOU START ACCUMULATING BUNDLES of flitch-cut veneers, you'll want to keep them organized and in good shape. Make sure to store them flat. If shipped in rolled form, let the sheets slowly relax, then number flitch-cut veneers sequentially to keep them in order. Wrap tape around the "end-grain" edges of each sheet to keep them from splitting. Highly figured veneers can be wavy and bumpy, and will need to be flattened before application to prevent cracking (see "Flattening Veneers," right).

Substrates and adhesives

COMMON SUBSTRATE MATERIALS include MDF, cabinet-grade particleboard, or high-quality plywood such as Italian poplar or Baltic birch. Bending plywood is useful for creating curved panels. Whatever substrate you choose should have a stable core and a smooth surface free of voids, bumps, and other irregularities. Avoid regular particleboard and other common building materials like construction-grade plywood. I also steer away from solid lumber as a substrate because of its seasonal wood movement.

UREA-FORMALDEHYDE (plastic resin) glue is one of the best adhesives

Flattening Veneers

To prevent buckling and cracking, burl and other lumpy veneers must be softened with a flattening agent and pressed before use. Commercial softeners work well, or you can brew your own concoction from two parts white PVA glue, one part glycerin, one part alcohol, and three-to-four parts water. Using a spray bottle or paint brush, soak both sides of the veneers. Repeat the process to keep them wet for a half hour. Then stack several sheets together, separating each with a few sheets of ink-free newsprint (available at art supply stores). Place the stack between plywood panels and apply light pressure. After 30 minutes, replace the newsprint. Change the paper every hour or two for eight hours, increasing the stack pressure as you go. Then maintain the pressure overnight.

for veneering, because it provides a long open time and dries very hard. However, it has to be mixed, and some health risks are associated with it. For many projects, I use polyvinyl acetate (PVA) or "yellow" glues like Titebond II and III. Both resist moisture, dry relatively hard, and suffer negligible "creep" over time. Titebond II can set up very quickly but is fine for smaller projects, while Titebond III allows longer open time for gluing up larger pieces. Other good choices include epoxy and Titebond Cold Press for Veneering. (I avoid contact cement, because the bond is unreliable.)

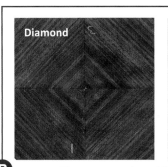

Diamond **X** **Cross** **Square diaper**

B These examples of four-way matches were all made using squares of macassar ebony veneer.

Shooting jig (1); layout tools (2); veneer tape and blue masking tape (3); scraper (4); scissors, saws, and knives (5); sanding sticks (6).

Tools and tapes

VENEERING REQUIRES MINIMAL GEAR (Photo C). Layout tools should include a drafting triangle for marking out square cuts and a protractor for laying out wedge-shaped matches. Scissors will rough-cut single sheets of veneer, while a veneer saw guided by a hardwood straightedge allows accurate cutting of several sheets at a time. I use knives for inlay and other intricate work. Shop-made sanding sticks (80 and 120 grit) are needed to shoot straight veneer seams, and a scraper will clean tape and glue from the veneered surface.

FOR CLEANER SAWING, I suggest modifying a standard veneer saw as shown in **Photo D**. Don't bevel the "underside," which rides against a straightedge when cutting.

FOR JOINING VENEERS, I use two types of tape: blue painter's tape and white veneer tape. The blue tape, which removes easily without leaving residue, is for temporarily attaching pieces during pattern matching. The paper veneer tape (sold by most veneer suppliers) is used for final attachment at the seams. It has water-activated glue on one side, making it easy to apply and remove without damaging the veneer. Immediately after applying the tape, dry it quickly with an iron, which also prevents excess moisture from swelling the wood fibers. Veneer tape is available either with holes to allow you to see the underlying seam or without holes for additional strength.

Gluing and clamping

TO APPLY VENEER TO A SUBSTRATE, first make sure to remove any blue tape from the underside of the veneer (having used it to temporarily align the pieces during layup). Then use a brush or short-nap paint roller to apply glue to the substrate (Photo E). Thoroughly coat the surface without soaking it. (Too much glue causes lumps, while a glue-starved surface can result in sections of the veneer lifting.) Press the dry veneer sheet onto the glued surface, and then immediately dampen it with distilled water to prevent curling. Wrap the edge of the assembly with blue tape to prevent shifting, and then cover the veneer with newsprint in preparation for clamping.

METHODS FOR CLAMPING, or *pressing*, the veneer to the substrate include vacuum clamping, screw-press clamping, and caul clamping. A vacuum press is a bag attached to a pump that evacuates the air from the bag to allow 14.7 pounds per

Hold a fine mill file at 5° to 10° to bevel the top edges of a veneer saw's teeth for clean cutting.

Roll out an even glue coat on the substrate. Keep blue tape, clamps, cauls, and platens handy to quickly clamp up the work before the glue dries.

Cover the faces of the glued-up panel with newsprint; then clamp the assembly between ¾" thick MDF platens, using cauls to distribute clamping pressure.

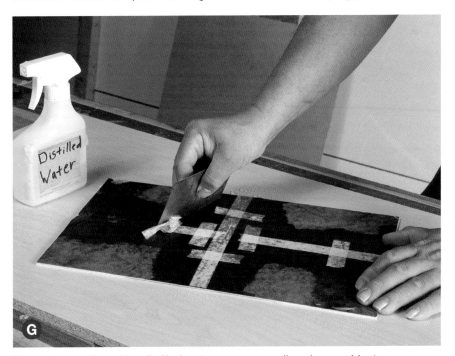

Veneer tape softened by distilled water removes easily using a cabinet scraper.

Sources

B&B Rare Woods: (303) 986-2585, *wood-veneers.com*

Certainly Wood: (716) 655-0206, *certainlywood.com*

Constantine's: (800) 443-9667, *constantines.com*

square foot of atmospheric pressure to press the veneer in place. This method is ideal for curved work. A screw-press applies pressure from above via clamping screws attached to an overhead frame. For smaller jobs, you can clamp the work between MDF platens, using long wooden cauls to spread pressure across the panel, as shown in **Photo F**. To ensure a good glue bond, leave the assembly clamped up for at least two hours.

Finishing up

AFTER THE GLUE HAS DRIED,

remove the veneer tape and scrape away any excess glue before sanding the surface. To remove the tape, spritz it with distilled water and let it sit for a few minutes before peeling away the softened tape with a cabinet scraper **(Photo G)**.

AFTER THE WATER EVAPORATES,

check the panel for "blisters" or other raised areas as described in "Fixing Veneer Blisters," at left. Make any needed repairs, and then scrape the entire surface of the panel with a sharp cabinet scraper to remove glue that may have squeezed through the veneer under clamping pressure. (Using sandpaper for this step risks cutting through the veneer.) After scraping, sand the surface with 220 grit before applying a finish. Surface-film finishes like lacquer, shellac, and varnish are good choices, because they overlay the veneer, unlike thin penetrating finishes like oils.

Fixing Veneer Blisters

In spite of your best efforts, "blisters" and other lifted areas can appear after you take a veneered panel out of its clamps. Check for lifted areas by lightly running your fingertips across the veneer while listening for any change in pitch. To repair a blister, slice into it at its edge, holding the knife at a steep angle away from the blister. Then inject glue into the cut under the loose area and reclamp the panel.

Laying Up a 4-way Match

THIS SIMPLE EXERCISE walks you through the basics of matching, sawing, and assembling veneers to create a "four-way" match panel, like the one shown at left. Here, I'm using four pieces of walnut burl veneer taken in sequential order from a flitch.

1 WITH THE SHEETS STACKED in their original sequence, number them from top to bottom, and then wrap blue painter's tape around the edges in several places to keep the stack intact during layout and cutting. Lay out a match using two ⅛" thick mirrors set square to each other. Tape their rear edges together and use a grooved panel to capture the top edges **(Photo H)**. (My panel is grooved at various angles to lay out 4-, 8-, 12-, and 16-way matches.) Shift the mirrors around on the veneer to preview a variety of layout options. Once you find the match you like, mark out the rough outlines by tracing along the mirrors.

2 GUIDING A VENEER SAW along a wooden straightedge, saw through the stack of veneers, cutting about 1/16" shy of your layout line **(Photo I)**. Hold the straightedge down firmly while pressing the

> **TIP ALERT**
> For better visibility, use a white pencil when marking dark veneers.

bottom of the saw against its edge. Make a series of light passes until each offcut separates from the sheet. Once you've cut through all the sheets, tape the sawn edge for stability, and then cut just shy of your second layout line in the same manner.

3 JOINT, OR *SHOOT,* one of the edges of the sawn stack straight to create gap-free seams. I use a straight-edged clamping jig, as shown in **Photo J**, but you can simply place the stack of veneers between two boards clamped in a vise. Align the upper edges of the boards with one of the two cutlines you drew during the mirror layout process and plane or sand away the projecting veneer edges flush with the edges of the boards. For tear-out-prone woods, I

prefer to use sanding sticks instead of a hand plane. I begin with 80 grit; then follow up with 120 grit.

4 UNTAPE THE PACKAGE and renumber the sheets in sequence if the original numbers were lost to the saw. Then lay out sheets 1 and 2 in paired form, flipping one sheet over to create a mirrored "book-match" with the jointed edges abutting. Do the same with sheets 3 and 4. With the "show" faces down, use a few short pieces of blue painter's tape to hold the seams together **(Photo K)**.

5 FLIP EACH TAPED PAIR over and check the seam alignment and the grain match, making alignment adjustments or reshooting if necessary. When the match is balanced and the seam tight, apply wet veneer tape to the show faces, as shown in **Photo L**. Briefly apply high heat from an iron to the tape to dry it. Then remove the blue tape from the back.

6 NOW PREPARE THE SEAM for joining the two pairs. First, tape them together at the edges, with the show face on the inside of the package and the previously joined seams precisely aligned, one on top of the other. Register one edge of a drafting triangle against the previously joined seam, and extend a cutline along the adjacent edge **(Photo M)**. Then repeat the procedure across the other half.

7 AGAIN USING A STRAIGHTEDGE as a guide, saw to your cutline. With the pieces still taped together, shoot the edge as before. Remove the tape and place the two assemblies together, show faces down with all four seams intersecting at the center. Use pieces of blue tape to connect the seams, and then flip the panel over to inspect the front for a symmetrical match. If either seam needs additional work, reshoot both edges, removing the same amount of material to maintain the pattern symmetry. When everything looks good, tape the seams on the show side with wet veneer tape as before **(Photo N)** and remove any remaining blue tape from the back. The "laid-up" sheet of veneer is now ready to be glued to a substrate.

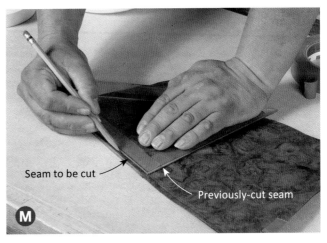

Seam to be cut

Previously-cut seam

COUNTRY-LOVING SALT BOX

This contemporary version of Samuel Plank's nineteenth-century salt box fits right in to the twenty-first-century kitchen, ready to store lots of things besides salt.

By Scott Phillips

Back in the 1880s in Pennsylvania farm country, a quiet group of Mennonite families crafted their way into woodworking fame. The most notable among them, the Samuel Plank family, made the finest wooden items to be found in the area. Their best seller was an item used to store salt on the wall near the stove. The dry heat coming off the stove helped keep the salt granular instead of lumpy. These so-called "salt boxes" sold for one to two dollars then. Today, authentic decorated antique salt boxes go for thousands.

Over a century later I became friends with Samuel's great-great-grandson, Doug Plank. Before long we were conspiring to build a "new use" salt box, one inspired by his ancestor. New use could mean storing anything from microwave popcorn packets to CDs to fire-starting materials to whatever. But keep in mind that by making it out of basswood, it is still perfect for kitchen use. Why? Simple: basswood is just about the only wood that never imparts odors or resins to food. Plus basswood has a quality that makes it the finest of all carving woods. It cuts easily and yet holds detail well. It's also an ideal project for using chip carving tools and creating original design.

I recommend that your first boxes be painted on the outside with milk paint for that antique look. The color should be personalized to match the use and the décor. Folk art additions are entirely fitting to this design. So make your mark and get creative!

Finally, you'll find this design a very easy one-day project, minus any special hand-painted or chip-carved embellishments. Note that the bottom drawer is "doubled up" to hold bigger items. The salt box originally had two smaller drawers used for storing spices and other kitchen items. To me one big drawer just works better. Here now is how to build it. You can also see the salt box online at *WBGU.org/AmericanWoodshop.*

A

B

Start with the right materials

1 THE MATERIALS LIST on page 61 shows you all the boards and hardware needed. So begin by carefully selecting ½" thick S4S basswood boards that are wide enough to avoid doing glueups. Really the only necessary glueup is for the scrolled box back.

Glue up a broad back and cut it to shape

1 FROM ½" BASSWOOD, edge-join enough stock (two to three pieces) to make a 14" wide × 16" long panel. Joint the edges, and then edge-glue the pieces with yellow woodworker's glue to make a flat panel. (The original salt boxes relied on hide glue and 1½" long finish nails and are still perfect more than a century later!)

2 NEXT, MAKE TWO COPIES of the full-sized half pattern (page 63), cut them out, and tape them together to make one full-sized pattern. Then, cut a scrap piece of Masonite, hardboard, or thin plywood to 14" × 16", the same size as the blank glueup for the box back. Apply the pattern flush at one end and two edges of the scrap piece and scroll saw this "template" to shape. Now, lay the template on the back panel and scribe the pattern's outline on it. Bandsaw or scroll saw the back to shape. We used a ³/₁₆" scrolling blade supported by Cool Blocks **(Photo A)**. Be sure to cut just to the outside of the cutline, and then sand

to the line to remove the saw marks and establish clean, crisp, curved edges. Set this valuable template aside for making more boxes later.

3 NOTE, TOO, THAT BY TRANSFERRING THE PATTERN so the grain runs vertically (as shown on the long 16" length) you create a strong hanger when installing the box on a wall. Do otherwise, and you risk snapping off the narrow neck of the back across a grain line when hanging or loading the box. With the patterned back cut, drill the ½" hanging hole where shown on the pattern.

Make the angled box sides

1 SAW THE BOX SIDES to the overall dimensions in the Cut List. (I used a miter sled for this; you can either build or buy one. Mine allows me to adjust the fence to make 90° and angle cuts.) Label one edge of each side the back edge and one end the top end. Now, measure 2½" in from each back edge and mark this location on the top ends of the sides. If you are not going to use a sled, then attach an auxiliary fence to your miter gauge. Then angle the fence to 12° and angle-cut the top ends of the sides, beginning at the 2½" mark or cutline **(Photo B)**. Hold the pieces together to see if they mirror each other. A poor match could result in sloppy fit later when the lid is added. Note: one way to ensure identical cuts is to tape the pieces face-to-face with double-faced tape and cut them together.

Machine the fixed top and beveled parts

1 CUT THE BOX'S FIXED TOP, lid, and front to the sizes in the Cut List. Note that the back edge of the lid and the top edge of the front have a 12° angle. To cut these, angle the blade, adjust the tablesaw fence to the needed width for that part, and make the cut as shown below.

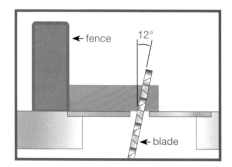

Cut the box divider and bottom

1 ADJUST THE SAW FENCE and blade and cut the box shelf and bottom to the sizes in the Cut List. Using a ½" roundover bit, rout the top ends and top front edge of the bottom.

Assemble a true and sturdy box

1 BEFORE ATTACHING THE SIDES TO THE BACK, make an assembly spacing jig to help hold the workpieces

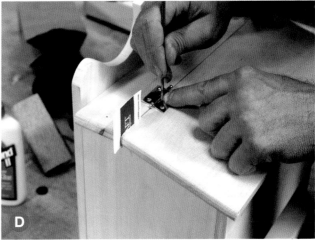

in place during nailing. Begin by cutting a 13" long piece from a 2 × 6. Cut out a 14" long piece from a scrap 2 × 10 to serve as the jig's base. Screw the top 2 × 6 in place onto the jig base allowing for a ½" offset along two ends and one edge. (The boards must be flat to work properly.) Also, cut two ½" thick scrap pieces to 7" wide and one to 13" wide to "box in" the sides and back during assembly and nail them to the base. Test-fit the sides and back in the jig by wedging them in the ½" gap **(Photo C)**. Next, predrill through the back and into the sides to create pilot holes for 1½" long finish nails. Now, remove the pieces, add glue along their joining edges, and slip them back into the jig to hold them in place. Drive the nails. It seems simple, but the jig really does help keep everything square. And if it does not stay square, well, you'll know, especially when the time comes to slip the drawer in place.

Add the fixed top, front, shelf, lid, and bottom

1 **CONTINUE THE BOX ASSEMBLY** by gluing and nailing on the fixed top and front. Using a small square and pencil, draw opposing guidelines on the inside walls of the box from the bottom edge of the front. These should be perpendicular to the front edges of the sides. Now, test-fit the shelf inside the box, aligning the ends with the

guidelines and one edge with the bottom edge of the front. Draw a guideline along the back edge, remove the shelf, apply glue along the guidelines, then fit it back in place. Drill pilot holes and drive in a few nails to hold in place.

2 **NEXT, APPLY A PAIR OF 1½" X 1¼" HINGES** to the fixed top. Using business cards as spacers in the seam between the lid and fixed top, center and screw the remaining hinge leaves atop the beveled edge of the lid **(Photo D)**.

3 **FINALLY, REST THE BOX ON ITS BACK** and center the bottom on the box. You should have a ½" offset at both ends and along the front edge. If the bottom is flat and the alignment is even, you're home free with the assembly. Note that there is no offset on the back of the salt box because you want the box to hang flat on the wall for the best look. With the bottom clamped in place, drill pilot holes for finish nails. Now, apply glue to the bottom edges of the box and drive three finish nails in each side.

Build a solid drawer frame

1 **CUT THE DRAWER FRONT,** back, and sides to the sizes in the Cut List. Cut the ½" rabbets ¼" deep on the ends of the sides using the crosscut sled or a miter gauge with an auxiliary fence and a ½" wide dado set. Don't have a dado set? No problem. Just

mark ½" in from the end of the sides and make multiple passes with your ⅛" wide saw blade up to the mark. This technique requires you to securely hold the drawer sides flat to the sled or saw table with the workpiece held firmly to the fence.

2 **NOW, SWITCH TO A ¼" DADO BLADE** raised ¼" high. Adjust the fence as shown below and cut the grooves on the front and sides ¾" from the bottom edge. You can also do this with a ⅛" blade by adjusting the fence as needed to "sneak" up on the needed groove width. Test the fit with the plywood you intend to use for the drawer bottom. There should be very little play.

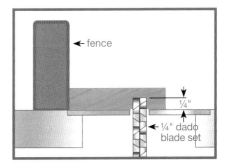

Slip in the drawer bottom

1 **DRILL A PAIR OF PILOT HOLES** 1" down from the top edge and 2¾" in from the ends of the front. Then, cut the plywood drawer bottom to size. Dry-fit the drawer box frame; check to see if the pieces fit in the drawer opening in the box. You should have about ¹⁄₁₆" clearance top and bottom.

Make any fine adjustments. Then glue and nail the pieces together, checking for square. You'll find that rabbet joints are so strong when glued that one nail per corner will do the job. Once the glue cures, a drawer this size should never fail. Slip in the drawer bottom from the back and tack it in place with a brad or two.

Make the false front

1 **CUT THE FALSE FRONT** to the sizes in the Cut List. With the drawer box sitting on a flat surface, center and clamp the false front to the drawer box front **(Photo E)**. Its top and bottom edges should be flush to the drawer front. Use the holes drilled earlier to drive #5 × ¾" round-head brass screws to hold the false front in place. Finally, drill centered holes through the false front and drawer front 3¼" in from each edge and add your pulls. Remove the pulls and sand the box with 220 grit in preparation for finishing.

Ease select edges to show wear

1 **TO ADD A RUSTIC,** used look to your salt box, break select outside edges with a low-angle block plane like the one shown in **Photo F.** These are must-have tools ideal for easing over any sharp edges prior to finishing. Sanding these edges often leads to dips in the edge that can be avoided if you use a hand plane.

Voilà! It's done.

I ONLY LEFT ⅛" OF PLAY FOR THE DRAWER ACTION. Then again, that's the way Mr. Plank would have wanted it. After all, he started this design over a century ago. Thanks for a fine design, Mr. Plank! Have fun! ✽

Country-Loving Salt Box Cut List

		Thickness	Width	Length
A	Scrolled box back, basswood	½"	14"	16"
B	Box sides (2), basswood	½"	7⅛"	9"
C	Fixed top, basswood	½"	2½"	15"
D	Lid, basswood	½"	5¾"	15"
E	Front, basswood	½"	5⅜"	14"
F	Divider/box shelf, basswood	½"	7⅛"	13"
G	Box bottom, basswood	½"	8½"	15"
H	Drawer front, basswood	½"	2½"	12⅜"
I	Drawer back, basswood	½"	1⅞"	12⅜"
J	Drawer sides (2), basswood	½"	2½"	7⅛"
K	Drawer bottom, plywood	¼"	6⅞"	12⁵⁄₁₆"
L	Drawer false front, basswood	½"	2½"	14"
	Jig base, 2x10	1½"	9½"	14"
	Jig core, 2x6	1½"	5½"	13"
	Jig sides (2)	½"	4"	7"
	Jig back	½"	4"	13"

MATERIALS

(2) Solid brass hinges, 1½" x 1¼"
(2) Porcelain/brass pulls of choice
(20) Finish nails, 4d 1½"
(2) Brads, ¾"
(2) Round-head brass wood screws, #5 x ¾"

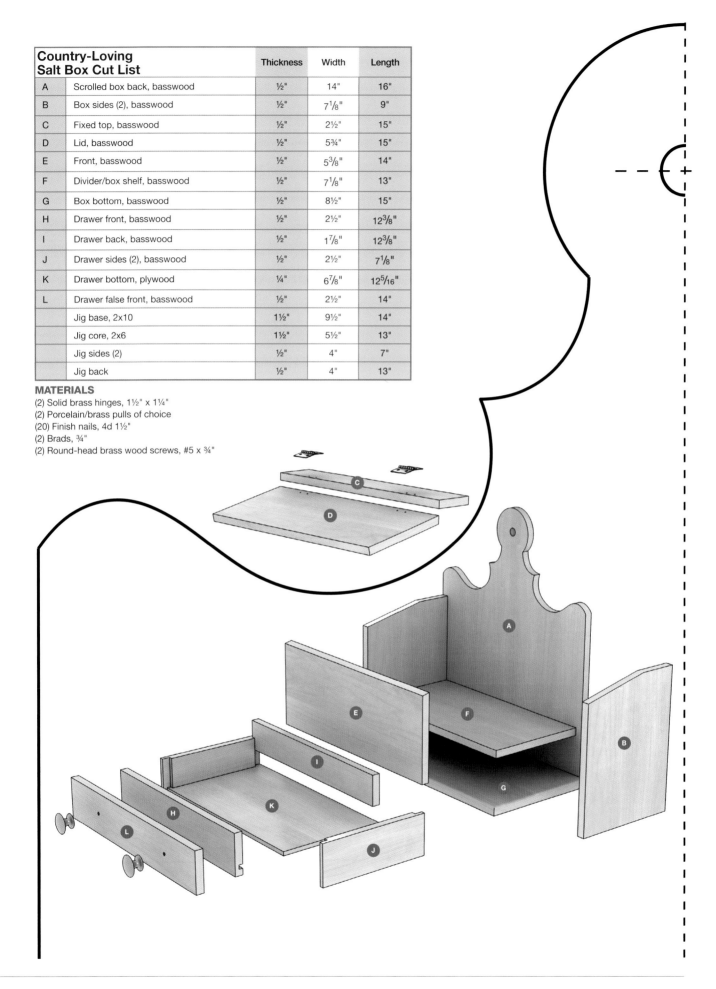

STEAK KNIVES & PRESENTATION BOX

Showcase special woods with this impressive matched set.

By Andy Rae

Here's a two-part project that's fun to make, and looks great below the yuletide tree. Both the steak knife handles and presentation box are made from a gorgeous Peruvian hardwood called orange agate (*platymiscium sp.*), which is a dense, tropical species from Peru. It cuts well with sharp tools, takes a beautiful polish, and holds up to moisture—a good choice for kitchenware. The box holds six knives, but can readily be scaled up or down to hold more or fewer knives.

A clever sliding lid snaps shut as if by magic thanks to two rare-earth magnets. The veneered lid, made from a figured piece of anigre, adds a nice contrast to the orange agate while letting you try your hand at simple veneering. Make the six knife handles first, so you can fit the box to the dimensions of the completed knives.

Overall dimensions: 2½" h × 12"d × 7³⁄₁₆"w

Fig. 1
KNIFE EXPLODED VIEW

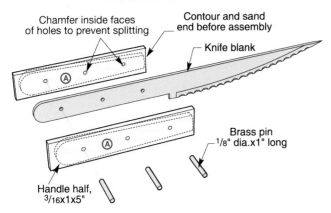

Chamfer inside faces of holes to prevent splitting

Contour and sand end before assembly

Knife blank

(A)

Brass pin 1/8" dia.x1" long

Handle half, 3/16x1x5"

Start with the knife handles

1 MILL A BLANK FOR THE SIX HANDLES, keeping it oversized in thickness and length, or about $5/8" \times 1" \times 32"$. To match the grain pattern for each handle, mark the edge of the stock for matching assemblies later, and then resaw the blank in half on a bandsaw or a tablesaw. The two resulting strips should be enough to make 12 handle halves (A) **(Figure 1)**. Thickness-plane the halves to 3/16" thick, making sure the inside faces are smooth and flat.

2 MARK THE KNIFE OUTLINES ON THE OUTSIDE FACE OF ONE HANDLE HALF, using a knife blank as a tracing template. Be sure to mark the hole locations on the stock, and label the individual blanks on this strip as well as its mate as shown in **Photo A**.

3 DRILL THE PIN HOLES IN THE HANDLE HALVES (A) ON THE DRILL PRESS, using a 1/8" brad-point bit. Use a scrap backer board underneath the stock to prevent blowing out the underside.

4 BANDSAW THE HANDLE HALVES (A) TO ROUGH SIZE, being careful to stay outside your marked lines. (You can substitute a scrollsaw if you like.) To prevent splitting when you drive the pins, chamfer around each hole on the inside face of each blank using a handheld countersink or a countersink bit chucked into the drill press.

5 FINISH-SAND THE FORWARD (BLADE) ENDS OF THE HANDLE BLANKS, sanding a gentle curve and rounding the end by hand with some 120-grit sandpaper wrapped around a block of wood. Sand through the grits up to 220, paying attention to any scratches or irregularities, as it will be hard to touch up this area after assembly.

Glue the blanks to the blades

1 CUT 18 PINS INTO 1" LENGTHS from a 1/8" diameter brass rod. To further prevent splitting the handle stock and to make installing the pins easier, bevel one end of each pin on a disc sander or with a fine file. Because the six pins for the forward holes in the knife blanks will be too tight to fit, you'll need to pre-size them. To do this, drive each pin partway through the hole by laying the blank over a makeshift anvil and striking the pin with a hammer as shown in **Photo B**. Now withdraw it.

2 GLUE THE HANDLE HALVES TO THE KNIFE BLANKS WITH TWO-PART EPOXY. Tape the cardboard sheath that comes with the knife blank to the blank, to protect your fingers from the blade. Before spreading the adhesive, tap all three pins through one handle half, beveled end down, until the beveled tips register in the holes in the knife blank. Then, spread epoxy on each handle half, position both halves over the knife blank, and tap the pins through all three parts, starting with the forward pin as shown in **Photos C** and **D**.

Trace the knife blank outline and its holes onto the outside face of one handle half. Label both halves for matching up later during assembly.

Use a pair of hand planes as a makeshift anvil to help you drive six pins through the forward holes of the knife blanks. Tap each pin about three-quarters of the way through the blank, then tap it back out.

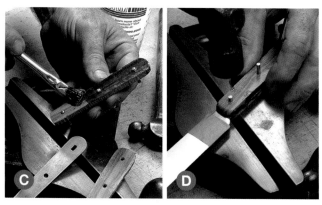

Tap the pins partway through one handle half, spread epoxy on both halves, position the parts together, and then drive the three pins through all three parts, beginning with the forward pin.

Clamp the handle halves to the knife blank using moderate clamping pressure. Wipe away excess epoxy from the knife blank by dampening a rag with denatured alcohol.

3 CLAMP THE ASSEMBLY AS SHOWN IN Photo E, WIPING AWAY EXCESS EPOXY on the knife blank with a clean rag dampened with denatured alcohol. Set the assembly aside to let the epoxy cure.

4 FILE OR SAND THE PINS FLUSH WITH THE HANDLE. Brass is relatively soft; a few swipes with a mill file, or a light touch on a stationary belt sander, should level the pins flush with the wood surface.

5 SAND THE HANDLE FLUSH WITH THE KNIFE BLANK, stopping when the edge of the knife blank is exposed. I used a stationary belt sander, but a mill file, followed up with some hand-sanding with 120-grit paper wrapped around a block of wood works just as well.

6 ROUND OVER THE EDGES OF THE HANDLE on the router table using a ⅛" round-over bit. To keep fingers safe, use a pushblock to move the workpiece, as shown in **Photo F.**

Finish the handles

1 FINISH-SAND THE HANDLES UP TO 220 GRIT, then use some 320-grit, wet-or-dry paper to smooth the face of the pins and the edges of the steel knife.

2 APPLY A HEAVY-DUTY FINISH so the handles will wear well in the kitchen. First, I applied a coat of dewaxed shellac to seal out any contaminants, smoothing the surface with a fine nylon abrasive pad once the finish had dried. Then I applied a few coats of a wipe-on polyurethane for maximum protection, using a small artist's brush to coat the forward ends to avoid getting any on the blade, and a rag for the rest. I let the handles dry as shown in **Photo G.**

Now for the presentation box

1 MILL THE SIDES (B), ENDS (C AND D,) AND THE PULL (E), referring to the **Cut List**. To keep the grain matched, mill the narrow end and the pull as one block of oversized wood, approximately ⅞" × 2⅝" × 7¼" then rip the block into

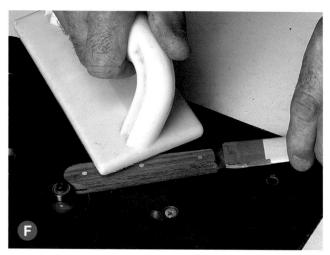

Keep fingers out of harm's way when rounding the edges. Cover the blade with a cardboard sheath and use a grippy pushblock to move the work.

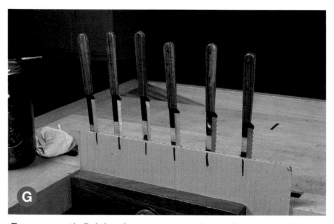

For a smooth finish, clamp a scrap piece of corrugated cardboard in a bench vise, then stick the knives into the cardboard while the finish dries.

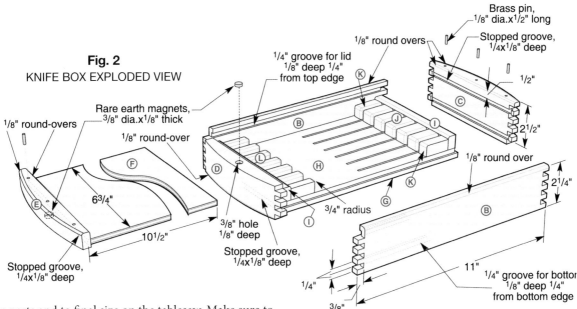

Fig. 2
KNIFE BOX EXPLODED VIEW

1/8" round-overs

Rare earth magnets, 3/8" dia.x1/8" thick

1/8" round-over

6 3/4"

10 1/2"

Stopped groove, 1/4x1/8" deep

1/4" groove for lid 1/8" deep 1/4" from top edge

1/8" round overs

Brass pin, 1/8" dia.x1/2" long

Stopped groove, 1/4x1/8" deep

1/2"

2 1/2"

3/8" hole 1/8" deep

Stopped groove, 1/4x1/8" deep

3/4" radius

1/8" round over

2 1/4"

1/4"

3/8"

11"

1/4" groove for bottom 1/8" deep 1/4" from bottom edge

---

separate parts and to final size on the tablesaw. Make sure to mark their orientation so you can put them back together in the correct order later.

2 CUT BOX JOINTS IN THE SIDES (B) AND ENDS (C AND D), making ¼" fingers and ¼" slots. Because orange agate is a brittle wood that is prone to chipping, I used a marking gauge to score lines around the stock before cutting the joints, which greatly reduces tear-out. To account for the difference in thickness between the sides and the ends, cut ³⁄₈" long fingers and slots in the end pieces, and ⅞" long joints in the sides as shown in **Photos H** and **I**.

3 CUT THE LID (F) AND BOTTOM (G) TO SIZE, referring to the **Cut List**. You can use regular hardwood plywood in a species of your choice, but to make the box really stand out, opt for a select veneer with ³⁄₁₆" thick solid stock (see "Veneering the Lid" on page 68).

4 ROUT THE GROOVES IN THE SIDES (B) AND ENDS (C AND D) for the lid (F) and the bottom (G), using a ¼" straight bit chucked in the table-mounted router. Align the grooves with the fingers and slots as shown in **Figure 2**. The

grooves are only ⅛" deep, which keeps the thin box sides strong. Cut through-grooves in the sides; then cut stopped grooves in the wider end (C) for both lid and bottom, and only one stopped groove in the narrow end (D) for the bottom only. Clamp stopblocks fore and aft of the bit on the table, and carefully lower the work onto the spinning bit as in **Photo J**. When the stock reaches the aft stopblock, carefully pivot the work up and away from the bit.

Note: You can cut the stopped groove for the bottom a tad longer than necessary, and then leave it as is since you won't see it after glue-up. The stopped groove for the lid, however, should stop precisely ⅛" past the joint's shoulder line. Once you've routed the grooves, square up the rounded ends on the lid groove with a small chisel. Check that the bottom sits securely in its grooves, and that the lid slides easily. Judicious sanding on the lid's underside will free it up for ideal sliding action.

5 CUT THE SHOULDERS ON THE SIDES (B) FOR THE LID PULL (E), removing one finger at one end of each side where shown in **Figure 2**. I used a handsaw to make this cut and cleaned it up with a chisel, but you could make the same cut using the miter gauge on the tablesaw.

Use a ¼" dado blade to cut ⅞" fingers in the sides and ³⁄₈" fingers in the ends.

Pivot the workpiece down and onto the bit and move it forward until it contacts the opposite stopblock.

Veneering the Lid

TO MAKE THE PRESENTATION BOX REALLY POP, veneer the lid from a wood of your choice. I chose highly figured anigre, an African wood that often displays tightly-packed curls across the grain, but practically any species will look great. Cut all your materials oversize, or about 7×11", as shown in **Figure 3**. You'll need four pieces of ¾" thick MDF (medium-density fiberboard) to act as cauls, two pieces of ¼" thick vinyl-coated hardboard to resist glue squeeze-out (you can substitute regular plywood instead if you give it a good coat of wax), plus a core of ⁵⁄₃₂" thick hardwood plywood with its face grain running opposite to the veneer.

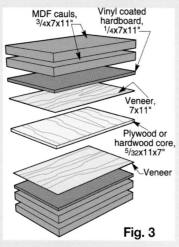

MDF cauls, 3/4x7x11"
Vinyl coated hardboard, 1/4x7x11"
Veneer, 7x11"
Plywood or hardwood core, 5/32x11x7"
Veneer

Fig. 3

Be sure to veneer both sides of the lid with the same or similar wood to stabilize the panel. Use a foam roller to place an even coat of regular white or yellow glue onto both faces of the core (never on the veneers), and then quickly position the veneers, core, hardboard, and cauls, and tape the package on each edge to avoid slippage.

Place the assembly over tall blocks. Then clamp from the center out. Once the glue has dried, level and smooth the surface by sanding with 120 grit up through 220, and then cut the lid to the finished dimensions in the **Cut List**.

Clamp the ends and the sides with bar clamps, checking that the assembly is square. Finish by clamping over the joints.

6 ROUND OVER THE SIDES (B) AND THE WIDER END (C), using a ⅛" round-over bit in the router table. For now, round over just the top inside and outside edges of the sides, stopping where they meet the wider end, and round over the top inside edge of the wider end (C). After assembly, round over the remaining edges, and finish up the stopped round-overs with chisels and careful sanding.

7 GLUE UP THE SIDES (B), ENDS (C AND D), AND BOTTOM (G), gluing the box joints as well as the plywood bottom. Clamp the ends first, then the sides, and check for square. When you're satisfied, place clamps directly over the box joints, using medium pressure to ensure the joints make good contact as shown in **Photo K**. Set the box aside on a flat surface to dry.

8 LAY OUT AND CUT THE CURVES ON THE ENDS (C AND D) AND PULL (E), using two copies of the pattern shown in **Figure 4**. First, adhere the pull (E) on top of the narrow end (D) with double-faced tape, and spray-adhere a copy of the pattern on the stack. Glue the second pattern to the top edge of the wide end (C). Now bandsaw the curves to shape. Clean up the saw marks on a stationary belt or disc sander, being careful not to over-cut or over-sand. You'll want to leave ⅜" long fingers on the sides for a consistent, symmetrical look. Now rout ⅛" round-overs on the top edges and ends of parts (C) and (E) as well as the outside bottom edges of the box.

9 INSTALL THE DECORATIVE PINS. Cut six ⅛" brass pins about ½" long. Use the pattern in **Figure 4** to lay out and mark exact pinhole locations in the box end and the pull. Drill the holes as before using a ⅛" brad-point bit on the drill press, making them about ⅜" deep. Apply epoxy to the pins then tap them into the holes. When the epoxy has cured, level the pins to the wood with a mill file or sanding block.

Fig. 4
FULL-SIZED PATTERN FOR ENDS

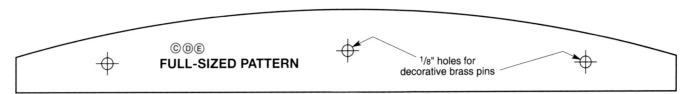

Ⓒ Ⓓ Ⓔ
FULL-SIZED PATTERN

1/8" holes for
decorative brass pins

Fig. 5
SLOT LAYOUT

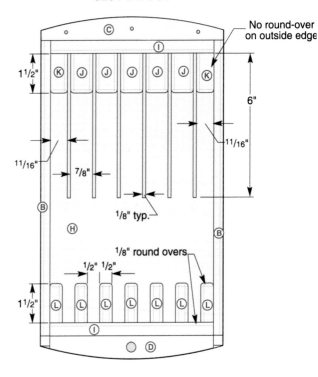

No round-over
on outside edge

Assemble the lid and pull

1 CUT A STOPPED RABBET IN THE PULL (E) ON THE ROUTER TABLE, again using a straight bit to make the cut. Raise the bit height ¼" and set the fence for a ⅛" cut. As before, set up stopblocks on both sides of the fence to limit the cut, stopping the cut ¼" from each end. Square up the rounded ends with a chisel.

2 GLUE THE PULL (E) TO THE LID (F), using a single bar clamp to draw the pull into the edge of the lid, and a couple of clamps to bring pressure down on top of the pull and onto the lid's face. Once the glue dries, check the fit of the lid in the box, and make any necessary adjustments. The lid should slide easily and close with the curved pull flush with the curved end of the box.

3 TO CREATE THE CLOSING SYSTEM FOR THE LID, lay out and mark the centered hole in the edge of the narrow box end (D) for the rare-earth magnet. Then lay out and mark the underside of the lid's pull, this time centering the hole along its length, but offsetting it $1/16$" towards the outside of the pull. This offset creates a pulling action when the lid is closed. Next, chuck a ⅜" Forstner bit in the drill press, and drill holes about ⅛" deep so the magnets sit slightly below the surface of the lid and box. Orient the magnets so they attract each other and epoxy them into their respective holes and let cure.

Divide the box interior

1 CUT THE SLOTTED BOTTOM (H) TO SIZE AND MILL THE END BLOCKS AND DIVIDERS (I, J, K, L) to the dimensions in the **Cut List**. Check the fit of the slotted bottom in the box, perhaps starting out oversized and then shaving its edges with a small plane for a precise fit.

2 NOW CUT THE SLOTS IN THE SLOTTED BOTTOM (H) ON THE TABLESAW, raising the blade to full height and adjusting the fence for each cut. Refer to **Figure 5** for the slot layout, and use a standard plywood-cutting blade to make the ⅛" wide slots. Clamp a stopblock to the far end of the saw fence as shown in **Photo L** on page 70 to stop the cut. Make sure to stop the saw each time to safely remove the panel for the next cut.

3 ROUND THE LEADING EDGES OF THE DIVIDERS (J, K, L), laying out the ¾" radii on one block and sawing it to shape on the bandsaw (see **Figure 4**). Clean up the saw marks and fair the curve on a stationary belt sander or by hand, and then use that divider to lay out and shape the remaining blocks.

4 ROUND OVER THE END BLOCKS (I) AND THE DIVIDERS (J, K, L), again using a ⅛" round-over bit in the router table. As before, use a pushblock to guide the small pieces past the spinning bit. Finish-sand all the blocks and dividers, as well as the slotted bottom, up to 220 grit.

5 INSTALL THE SLOTTED BOTTOM (H), placing a few beads of glue underneath and weighting the plywood down for a flat, solid bond.

6 GLUE AND CLAMP THE END BLOCKS (I) ON TOP OF THE SLOTTED PLYWOOD. Use only a moderate amount of glue to avoid squeeze-out.

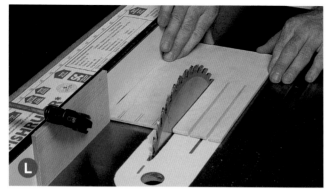

L

Layout marks on the plywood help set the fence for each cut. Raise the blade and push the part into the saw, stopping when the panel contacts the stopblock. Turn off the saw before removing the panel.

M

Arrange the dividers using scrap spacers, and then install them by pressing them in place with glue.

7 ATTACH THE DIVIDERS (J, K, L) TO THE BOTTOM WITH GLUE, using spacers to position them. I made spacers from scrapwood, using ½" wide spacers for the handle dividers and ⅛" wide spacers for the blade dividers. Arrange the blocks with the spacers to make sure they fit before spreading any glue, then apply glue to the end dividers first, and press them into position against the sides and down onto the plywood. Finish up by installing the remaining dividers, again coating them with glue and pressing them into place as shown in **Photo M**.

Finish the box

1 SAND THE BOX UP TO 220 GRIT and apply the finish of your choice. To keep the look in tune with the knives, I chose the same finish regimen that I used on the handles, although I didn't apply as many coats: one coat of shellac to seal the wood, followed by two coats of wipe-on poly.

2 RUB IT OUT FOR A BEAUTIFUL SHINE. When the finish has cured thoroughly (it takes about a week), rub out the entire box and the knife handles with paste wax to smooth the finish and protect the surface. Now, sign the box, fill it with the knives, and present it to someone special. 🪚

Cutting Diagram

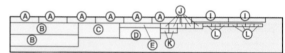

1"x6"x4' orange agate

¼" x 12" x 12" veneer plywood

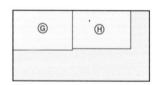

¼" x 12" x 12" maple plywood

Steak Knives & Presentation Box Cut List		Thickness	Width	Length	Qty.	Mat'l
Knives						
A	Handle halves	³⁄₁₆"	1"	5"	12	OA
Knife Box						
B*	Sides	⅜"	2¼"	12"	2	OA
C*	End	⅞"	2½"	7¼"	1	OA
D	Narrow End	⅞"	1¾"	7¼"	1	OA
E	Pull	⅞"	¾"	7¼"	1	OA
F	Lid	¼"	6¾"	10½"	1	VP
G	Bottom	¼"	6¾"	10½"	1	MP
Box Dividers						
H	Slotted bottom	¼"	6½"	10¼"	1	MP
I	End blocks	½"	¾"	6½"	2	M
J	Blade dividers	⅝"	⅞"	1½"	5	M
K	End blade dividers	⅝"	¹¹⁄₁₆"	1½"	2	M
L	Handle dividers	⅝"	½"	1½"	7	M

*Indicates a part that is initially cut larger; please see the instructions for details.
OA=Orange Agate M=Maple MP=Maple Plywood VP=Veneer Plywood

POST OFFICE BOX BANK

Post office box doors find new life in this easy weekend project.

By A. J. Hamler with Robert J. Settich

You've probably seen this style of bank before, cleverly made using old post office box doors, in gift shops and catalogs. But there's no need to pay retail when you can easily make the project yourself. As you'll see, not only are the banks easy and inexpensive to construct, the retired post office box doors are more available than you might think.

Now, after you build the first one and show it off, be warned that it carries a certain risk: You'll instantly get requests to make more. In fact, you'll probably end up with a substantial list of folks who want them as gifts. The good news is that this project lends itself to a production process that will help you turn out several banks at a time.

Overall dimensions: 4³⁄₈"w x 4¹⁄₂"d x 6³⁄₈"h

To cut rabbets at your router table, raise the bit in 1/8" increments to avoid chip-out, moving the work from right to left.

Begin with the sides, bottom, and back

1 JOINT AND PLANE A 16" LONG BOARD to ⅝" thick, and then rip it into a 4½" wide blank for the sides (A) and bottom (B).

2 USING A STRAIGHT BIT IN A TABLE-MOUNTED ROUTER, rout the dado along one edge of the blank as shown in **Photo A**. Note in **Figure 1** that this produces the rabbet in the rear inner edges of the sides (A) and bottom (B). For an alternative method, mount a dado head in your tablesaw, and attach a sacrificial plywood face to your rip fence. Adjust the blade and fence to produce a ⅜" × ⅜" rabbet, and then make the cut.

3 AT YOUR MITERSAW, SQUARE UP ONE END OF THE BLANK, and crosscut the sides (A) to the length in the **Cut List**. Using a stopblock and stacking the two sides, trimming them simultaneously ensures equal length. Initially cut the bottom (B) about ⅛" longer than indicated. (You'll trim it to final length after a test assembly.)

4 RESET YOUR TABLESAW SETUP to cut a ⅜" × ⅝" rabbet. Referring to **Figure 1**, cut this rabbet at the inside bottom end of each side (A). Use a square scrapwood pushblock to guide the part accurately and to keep fingers away from the blade. The pushblock also helps prevent tear-out where the cutter exits the wood.

5 CLAMP THE SIDES (A) to the bottom (B), and test-fit the door. The ideal is a smooth sliding fit that doesn't rattle side to side. Mark and trim the bottom to final length. Repeat the test-fitting to confirm your results.

6 LAY THE CLAMPED ASSEMBLY ON ITS BACK. Position the door with half the width of the upper frame overlapping the upper ends of the sides (A). Poke a pencil through the holes in the mounting tabs to transfer the locations to the inner face of the sides. Before unclamping the assembly, verify the size of the back (C).

7 AT YOUR DRILL PRESS, drill a 3/32" pilot hole ½" deep at each mounting tab location.

8 JOINT AND PLANE A 10" LONG PIECE OF STOCK to ⅜" thick for the back (C). Rip and crosscut to size, trimming away planer snipe.

9 GLUE AND CLAMP THE SIDES (A), bottom (B), and back (C). Referring to **Figure 1**, drive a pair of 4d (1½") finishing nails through the bottom and into each side. Slightly angle each nail toward the center of the side to improve its holding power.

Add the top

1 FROM 1" THICK STOCK, cut a piece to 4⅜" × 4½" for the top (D).

2 CENTER THE BRASS COIN SLOT ON THE TOP (D) and pencil the outline of the slot opening onto the wood. Chuck a

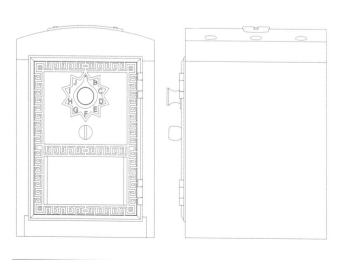

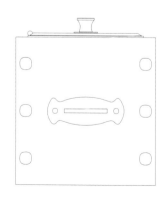

Fig. 1
POST OFFICE BOX EXPLODED VIEW

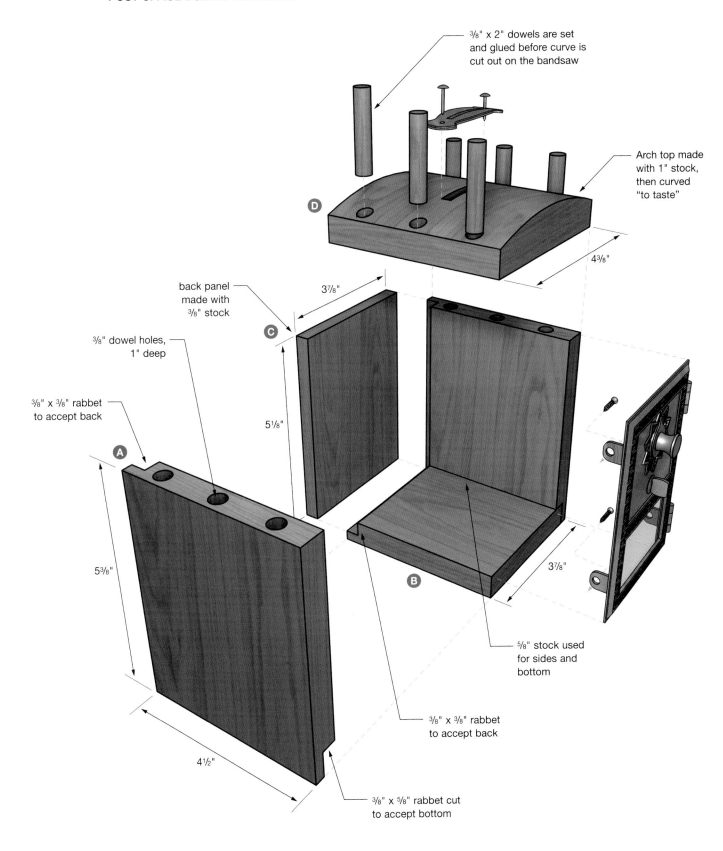

³⁄₈" x 2" dowels are set
and glued before curve is
cut out on the bandsaw

Arch top made
with 1" stock,
then curved
"to taste"

4³⁄₈"

3⁷⁄₈"

back panel
made with
³⁄₈" stock

Ⓓ

Ⓒ

³⁄₈" dowel holes,
1" deep

5¹⁄₈"

³⁄₈" x ³⁄₈" rabbet
to accept back

Ⓐ

5³⁄₈"

Ⓑ

3⁷⁄₈"

⁵⁄₈" stock used
for sides and
bottom

4¹⁄₂"

³⁄₈" x ³⁄₈" rabbet
to accept back

³⁄₈" x ⁵⁄₈" rabbet cut
to accept bottom

B

Use a minimal glue film on the dowels, otherwise excess fluid trapped in the hole could make it impossible to fully drive the pins in place.

¼" bit into your drill press, and clamp a fence to the table so you can drill a series of holes along the centerline of the slot. Don't make the slot too long, or you won't have a solid target for the escutcheon pins that attach the brass. Clean up the slot with a chisel.

3 CHUCK A ⅜" BRAD-POINT BIT INTO YOUR DRILL PRESS, clamp a fence to the table, and drill the dowel holes through the top (D) where shown in **Figure 1**.

4 CLAMP THE TOP (D) TO THE BOTTOM ASSEMBLY (A, B, C), carefully flushing the ends and edges of the parts, but leaving the holes accessible for further drilling. By using a single pipe or bar clamp at the center of the top, you can also clamp the entire assembly to the edge of your workbench.

5 CHUCK THE ⅜" BRAD-POINT BIT INTO A PORTABLE DRILL. Using the holes through the top (D) as guides, extend each hole 1" deep into the sides (A). Unclamp the assembly to clear chips from the holes. Be careful that you don't rotate or flip the top.

6 CUT A ⅜" DIAMETER DOWEL ROD INTO SIX PIECES 2" long. (Because the end of the dowels will be visible, do not use dowel pins with flutes or helical grooves.)

7 APPLY A THIN FILM OF GLUE TO THE MATING SURFACES, and put the top above the bottom assembly (A, B, C). With a toothpick, wipe glue onto the wall of each hole, and tap in the dowels as shown in **Photo B**. Wipe up excess glue, and ensure that the joints close tightly. Let the assembly dry.

8 LAY OUT THE CURVE ON THE FRONT EDGE OF THE TOP (D). There are several ways to accomplish this. To begin one method, lay the assembly on its back and tape a piece of plywood to the sides (A). Draw a centerline between the

Door Buying Advice

While you'll see several sources for post office box doors in the **Convenience-Plus Buying Guide**, you can also scour flea markets and online auctions. Although they are generally not rare items, several factors can affect the price for certain doors. For example, doors with a sculpted eagle or embossed "U.S." usually command a premium. Those with both elements are even more desirable. At the opposite end of the spectrum, doors that are corroded or have bent frames can be a false bargain at almost any price. Avoid them. Doors with key locks are considered less desirable than the combination style because having a locksmith create a key can be expensive.

You'll encounter a variety of door sizes, but the No. 1 size is the smallest and most plentiful. The dimensions of this project are based on a No. 1 Grecian door, which measures 3⅛" horizontally between the outer edges of the

mounting tabs, and 4¾" vertically (center to center of the rails). If your door has different dimensions, adjust the size of the parts for your bank. You'll also find a variety of door-frame mounting systems that may require modification to the procedure described here.

Of course, you'll want the door in hand before starting construction.

With your bandsaw table square to the blade, cut the arch just outside the line in the top of the bank assembly.

Avoid burn marks and gouges when disc-sanding by using a light touch, gently sweeping the bank's top against the disc.

sides, and set a compass to scribe a 5" radius. Referring to **Figure 1**, position the pivot point of the compass on the centerline so that the pencil strikes the end of the top about 7/16" above the upper end of the side (A). A simpler method involves tracing along the rim of a 10" diameter object, such as a dinner plate. If you use this method, ensure that the apex of the curve is at the center of the top's length.

9 **REFERRING TO PHOTO C,** bandsaw about 1/16" to the waste side of the marked line.

10 **SAND TO THE PENCIL LINE** to smooth the surface using a disc sander, as shown in **Photo D**. Do your sanding on the downhill side of the disc to ensure that the assembly stays flat on the table. After disc-sanding, do a final hand-sanding with the grain on all surfaces with 180 grit.

Time to finish

1 **REMOVE DUST FROM THE WOOD** by vacuuming or with a tack cloth. To accentuate the walnut's figure, wet the project with natural Watco Danish Oil finish. Over the next 15 minutes, apply more finish to areas that appear dry. Then scrub the wood with dry cloths to remove all the finish possible.

2 **NOW, CHOOSE TO APPLY ADDITIONAL COATS OF WATCO,** or, for a more durable film-forming finish, apply two coats of gloss Watco Wipe-On Polyurethane, followed by one coat of the satin version of that finish. To remove dust nibs between coats, lightly sand with 320 sandpaper, then wipe the surfaces with a tack cloth.

3 **FOR AN EVEN SATIN SURFACE,** I lightly rubbed the bank with 0000 steel wool. A final coat of paste wax brings out the sheen.

Rats! I Lost the Combination

IT HAPPENS. Despite your best precautions, you've forgotten the combination and lost the written backup. But you don't need to demolish the bank to open it. Lay the bank on its back, and put a center punch onto the glass. A sharp hammer rap or two should shatter the glass. Now you can reach a finger inside the bank and locate the horizontal locking plunger—it's just below the lower knob. Slide the plunger toward the hinge side to open the door. Remove the two screws that attach the cover plate over the combination mechanism, and you'll be able to quickly decipher the opening sequence. Record the number...again. Now replace the glass.

Use light finger pressure to bend the brass coin slot to match the bank's curved top. For ease of insertion, drill tiny pilot holes for the escutcheon pins.

Install the doors by using a stubby or offset screwdriver to drive the fasteners home.

Add the hardware

1 GENTLY BEND THE BRASS COIN SLOT with your fingers so it conforms to the top's arch, as shown in **Photo E.** Carefully align the slot, and use a scratch awl to transfer the hole locations to the top. Drill pilot holes for the escutcheon pins, and drive them.

2 BEFORE ATTACHING THE DOOR, write down the combination, and stash it where you can easily retrieve it.

3 POSITION THE DOOR (Photo F), and drive the screws to secure it. You can correct the door's fit by gently bending the mounting tabs with a pair of pliers. But work carefully, so you don't accidentally crack the casting.

4 ADD SELF-ADHESIVE FELT PADS to the bottom of the bank. 🪵

P.O. Box Bank Cut List		Thickness	Width	Length	Qty.	Mat'l
Box						
A	Sides	⁵⁄₈"	4¹⁄₂"	5³⁄₈"	2	W
B*	Bottom	⁵⁄₈"	4¹⁄₂"	3⁷⁄₈"	1	W
C*	Back	³⁄₈"	3⁷⁄₈"	5¹⁄₈"	1	W
D*	Top	1"	4¹⁄₂"	4³⁄₈"	1	W

* Initially cut part long. See instructions.
Material key: W = walnut
Hardware/Supplies: post office box door, brass coin slot with escutcheon pins, #6 x ¹⁄₂" roundhead screws, ³⁄₈" dowel rod, 4d (1¹⁄₂") finishing nails, ¹⁄₂" self-adhesive felt pads

Magic Coin Bank

Mystery and illusion via a tricky mirror

By Ken Burton

Overall dimensions: 8½"w × 8½"d × 8½"h

This fun and mysterious bank is sure to delight children of all ages. Coins dropped in the slot seem to disappear, leaving the box empty except for a small wooden cube which appears to float in the center. The secret to the illusion is an internal mirror set at a 45° angle, creating the impression that the bank is hollow, while the money drops into the section behind the mirror.

There's no magic to building this project, but you'll certainly learn some woodworking tricks. They include a great lesson in spline joinery, with hidden splines used to attach the case parts, and keyed splines used to join the mitered front and rear frames. The only specialty supplies involved are a "front-surface" mirror and a checkerboard-patterned paper liner for the interior. See the **Convenience-Plus Buying Guide** for the mirror source, and go to page 82 and 83 for the liner pattern.

I made this box from sassafras, which is relatively soft and easy to work with both hand and power tools. As an added bonus, freshly cut sassafras exudes a delightful, spicy aroma that will leave your shop smelling exotic for several days. However, you can use any wood of your choosing to build the bank. Although you could use glass for the front of the box, I chose to use acrylic to provide for child safety.

Fig. 1
MAGIC COIN BOX EXPLODED VIEW

⅜" rabbet,
⅛" deep

¼" coin slot
centered

1⅜"

⅛" spline slot,
⅜" deep

¼" groove,
¼" deep

³⁄₁₆" groove,
¹³⁄₃₂" deep

Paper liner

See retaining
strip detail

Spline

¼" × ½" flathead
woodscrew

6¹¹⁄₁₆" × 6¹¹⁄₁₆"
acrylic

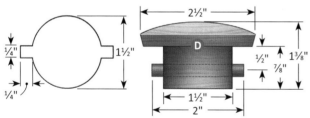
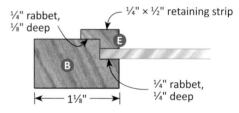

8" × 9⅝" front
surface mirror

⅛" spline slot,
1" deep

Spline

#6 × 1½" trim head
woodscrew

BACK HOLE AND PLUG DETAIL

2½"

1½"

¼"

¼"

½"

1⅜"

⅞"

1½"

2"

RETAINING STRIP DETAIL

¼" rabbet,
⅛" deep

¼" × ½" retaining strip

E

B

¼" rabbet,
¼" deep

1⅛"

Make the case

1 Mill a 36" length of stock for the box sides to the thickness and width shown in the **Cut List** (page 81). Then cut each individual side (A) about ⅛" oversized in length for now. Mark the mating ends for reassembly later in their original sequence to ensure grain continuity around the box. Orient the one mismatched corner to be on the underside; then mark the top piece to identify it as such.

2 Tilt the blade on your tablesaw to 45°, and miter one end of each side (A). Use a stop on your miter gauge fence to help keep the pieces from slipping as you cut. Reset the stop to cut the pieces to final length while mitering the other ends, as shown in **Photo A**.

Stop

A

Miter the ends of the box sides so the waste is located under the leaning blade, not above it.

Adjust the fence and blade height to cut the ³⁄₈" deep spline slots ¹⁄₈" in from the inside edge of the miter.

Cut the coin slot on the router table in two passes, using stopblocks to limit the slot's length.

3 **WITH THE SAW BLADE STILL** tilted at 45°, position your rip fence to cut the ³⁄₈" deep spline slots in the mitered ends, where shown in

Figure 1. Guide the mitered ends along the fence to make the cuts as shown in **Photo B.**

4 **CUT A PIECE OF ³⁄₄" THICK STOCK** to 2¼" wide × 18" long to use as spline stock. Then use scrap to set up the saw for a ¹⁄₈" thick rip that creates a snug fit in your spline slots. With that saw setting, resaw two lengths of 2¼" wide stock from your 18" long piece; then crosscut 12 pieces ¹¹⁄₁₆" long from that to use as case splines. Save the rest of the material for the frame splines to be made later.

Sawing the Grooves

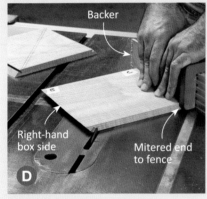

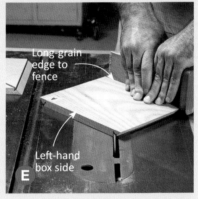

Saw the ¹³⁄₃₂" deep grooves for the mirror. Set the miter gauge at 45° to the blade, and use the same stop position for both opposing cuts. Cut the right-hand piece with its end against the fence and the left-hand piece with its side against the fence.

5 **CHUCK A ¼" STRAIGHT BIT IN YOUR TABLE-MOUNTED ROUTER,** and cut the coin slot, centering it in the top piece as shown in **Photo C.**

6 **LAY OUT THE GROOVES FOR THE MIRROR ON THE TWO OPPOSING BOX SIDES** (A), as shown in **Figure 2.** Make the cuts on the tablesaw, as shown in **Photos D** and **E.** You can use the same stop setting for both pieces, but you'll need to load the pieces onto the miter gauge in two different orientations. On one piece, the mitered end rests against the fence, and on the other, the side goes against the fence. Use a plywood backer to minimize exit tear-out. After making both initial cuts, reposition the stop and make a second pass on each piece to widen the cuts to ³⁄₁₆".

7 **MAKE UP FOUR 7 × 8" CLAMPING CAULS** from scraps of ¼" thick plywood with 45° strips glued and screwed at either end. Clamp the cauls to the sides;

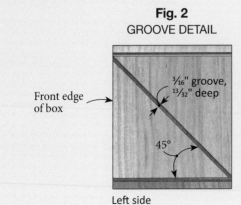

Fig. 2
GROOVE DETAIL

Grooves should run from corner to corner.

Front edge of box

³⁄₁₆" groove, ¹³⁄₃₂" deep

45°

Left side

Right side

Glue triangular strips to scrap plywood; then clamp across the box corners to close the miter joints.

then dry-fit the four sides together, as shown in **Photo F.** When you are happy with the fit, glue the box together.

Make the frames

1 CUT THE FRONT AND BACK FRAME pieces (B) about $1/16$" longer than the sizes shown in the **Cut List**. This will create slightly oversized frames that you'll trim flush to the case after assembly.

2 USING A MITER GAUGE AND STOP, miter the ends of the pieces to 45°. Glue four of the pieces together to make up the front frame, as shown in **Photo G.**

3 CUT CENTERED $1/4$" WIDE × $1/4$" DEEP GROOVES in the remaining four frame pieces, where shown in **Figure 1,** to accept the back panel (C).

4 CUT A PIECE OF STOCK FOR THE BACK PANEL to the size shown in the **Cut List**. Saw or rout $3/8$" wide rabbets in the edges to create tongues that fit in the rear frame grooves.

5 DRILL A $1½$" DIAMETER HOLE THROUGH THE CENTER OF THE BACK PANEL. Then use a coping saw to cut opposing notches at the perimeter, as shown in the **Back Hole and Plug Detail** in **Figure 1.**

6 GLUE THE BACK FRAME TOGETHER as you did with the front frame. Be sure to slip the back panel (C) in its grooves before clamping the pieces (B) together.

7 TURN A $1½$" DIAMETER PLUG (D) with a $7/8$" long spigot, as shown in the **Back Hole and Plug Detail** in **Figure 1.** (If you don't have a thick enough piece of sassafras, either glue up thinner pieces or use another species such as oak.) Test the fit of the spigot in its hole. Drill a $1/4$" diameter hole through the spigot, and glue a 2" length of $1/4$" diameter dowel in place to serve as a lock.

8 WITH THE BLADE RAISED 1", saw centered spline slots in the corners of both frames by carrying each across the blade at a 45° angle, using a jig like the one shown in **Photo H.**

9 CUT THE PREVIOUSLY UNUSED SPLINE MATERIAL into slightly oversized triangular splines to fit in the slots. Swab the pieces with glue, and tap them home, as shown in **Photo I.** When dry, trim the splines flush with a chisel and block plane.

10 ROUT A $1/4$" WIDE × $1/4$" DEEP RABBET around the inside of the front frame, and then square the corners with a chisel.

11 MAKE THE RETAINING STRIPS (E) THAT HOLD IN THE ACRYLIC PANEL, as shown in the **Retaining Strip Detail** in **Figure 1.** The best approach here is to saw or rout the $1/8$" × $1/4$" rabbet in the edge of a $1/2$" thick board; then rip the $1/4$" wide retaining strip from the rabbeted edge. Crosscut the strips to the lengths shown in the **Cut List;** then miter the pieces to fit the rabbet in the front frame.

Assemble and finish the box

1 GLUE THE BACK FRAME to the back of the box.

2 PRINT OUT THE LINERS ON COVER STOCK or other heavy paper, and trim them to fit inside the box. If you need to make the pieces smaller,

Glue up the front frame with a band clamp or self-squaring frame clamp, like the one shown here.

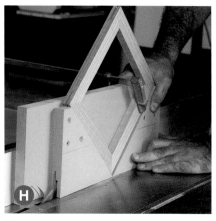

Make a simple V-shaped carrier to hold the frames for sawing the spline slots in the corners.

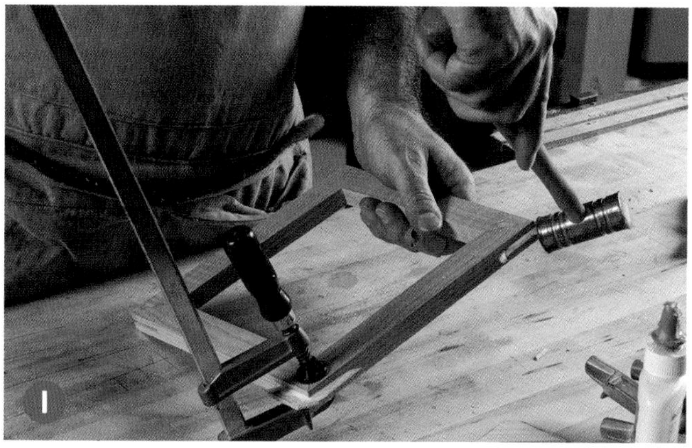

Glue the splines into their slots, and then tap them home to fully seat them before clamping at the frame corners.

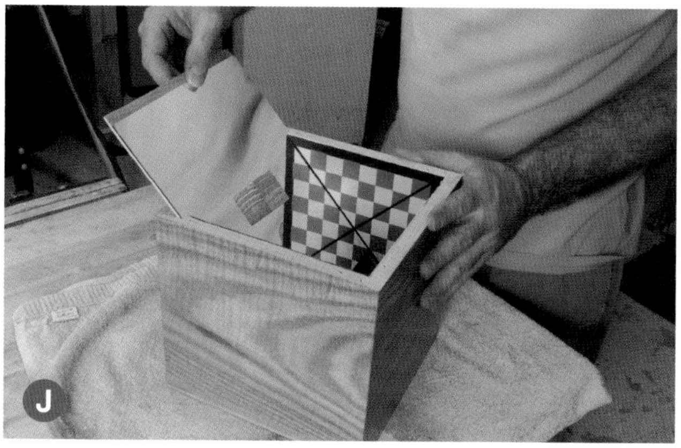

To avoid breaking the mirror, carefully slide both it and the backer into the box grooves at the same time.

trim an equal amount off each side to keep the borders an even width. Brush rubber cement on the back side of the liner pieces and on the inside surfaces of the box and allow it to dry. Then carefully adhere the liners to the inside of the box.

3 CUT THE MIRROR TO 8 × 9 5/8". *Note: This mirror is very thin. To avoid cracking it, handle it carefully when removing the protective plastic covering and when cutting it.*

4 SAW THE ACRYLIC TO 6 11/16" × 6 11/16". A standard carbide combination blade on the tablesaw will do the job fine.

5 CUT THE FLOATING BLOCK (F) TO THE SIZE SHOWN in the **Cut List**, using quartersawn material so the grain pattern doesn't spoil the illusion in the mirror (see **Figure 1**). Finish the block with shellac; then affix it to the mirror at its center, using cyanoacrylate (CA) glue.

TIP ALERT

Instruction on cutting mirror is available on the Internet, including a lesson at ***wikihow.com/Cut-Glass.*** Or, your local glass supplier will usually do the job for you at minimal cost.

6 CUT A PIECE OF 1/8" THICK PLYWOOD to 8 × 9 5/8" to serve as a backer (G) for the mirror. Then carefully slip the backer and mirror into their grooves at the same time, as shown in **Photo J**.

7 PLACE THE ACRYLIC IN ITS RABBETS in the front frame, and then attach the retaining strips (E) to the frame using #4 × ½" wood screws. Clean the inside surface of the acrylic thoroughly.

8 SCREW THE FRONT FRAME TO THE BOX with eight #6 × 1½" trim head screws. Plane, scrape, and sand the edges of both frames to flush them to the box sides. Then sand the whole box through 220 grit.

9 TEMPORARILY APPLY MASKING TAPE TO THE ACRYLIC TO PROTECT IT, and then apply several coats of your favorite wood finish. I used spray shellac.

Convenience-PLUS BUYING GUIDE	
	ITEM
☐ 1.	**Whiteside Straight Bit, ¼" D, ¾" CL (¼" SH)**
☐ 2.	**Whiteside Rabbeting Bit Set, (½" SH)**
☐ 3.	**Self Squaring Frame Clamp**
☐ 4.	**Acrylic, 1/8"-thick**
Above item available at home supply centers.	
☐ 5.	**8 × 12" Front Surface Mirror, 1/16" thick**
Above item available from Glass Crafters Stained Glass at glasscrafters.biz or by calling (800) 422-4552.	

Magic Coin Bank Cut List		Thickness	Width	Length	Qty.	Mat'l
A*	Sides	5/8"	7¼"	8½"	4	S
B*	Frame pieces	5/8"	1 1/8"	8½"	8	S
C	Back panel	3/8"	6 11/16"	6 11/16"	1	S
D*	Plug	1 3/8"	2½" diameter		1	S
E*	Retaining strips	¼"	½"	7¼"	4	S
F	Floating block	5/8"	1¼"	1¼"	1	QO
G	Mirror backer	1/8"	8"	9 5/8"	1	P

*Indicates parts that are initially cut oversized. See instructions.
** Indicates parts that are undersized by 1/32"
Materials: VPly=Maple Veneered over Baltic Birch Plywood, C=Cherry; M=Maple, Ply=Baltic Birch Plywood
Supplies: (8) #4 × ¾" flathead wood screws for attaching top, (8) #6 × ¾" roundhead wood screws for attaching the false fronts.

PATTERNS

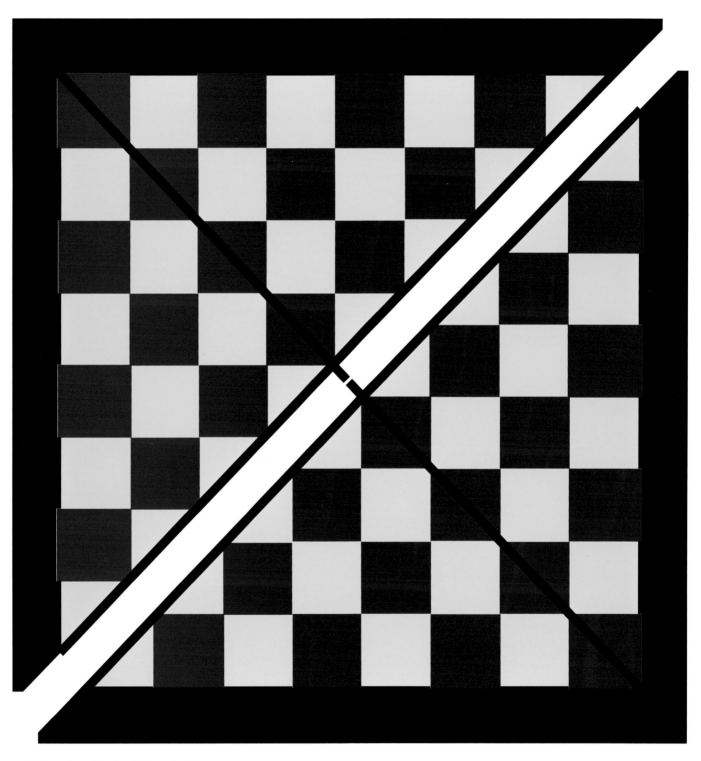

Magic Coin Bank Box
page 77

Patterns full size

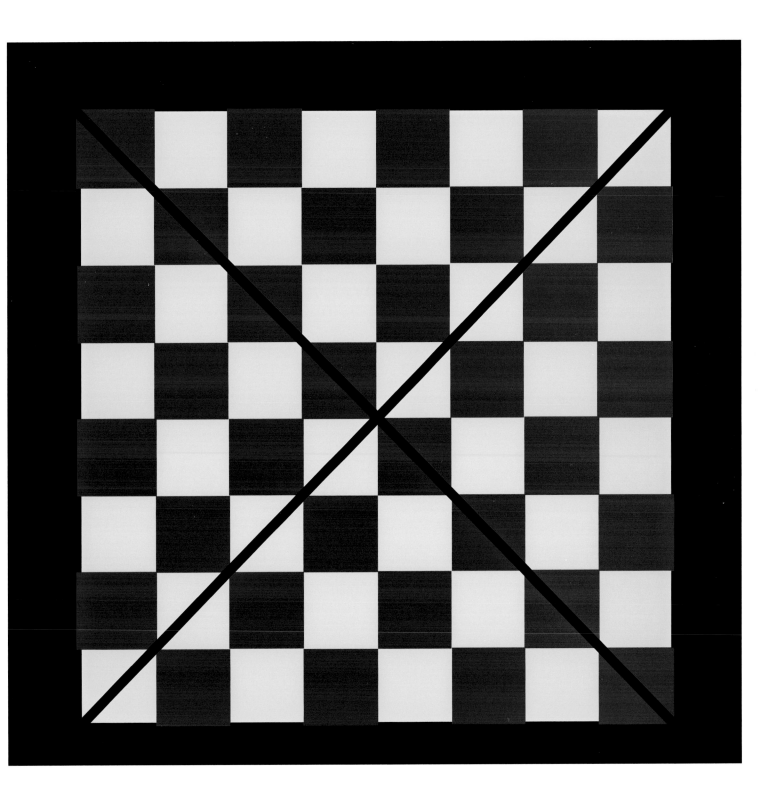

Eye-catching wood color/grain combos: from left, veneered box (walnut, cherry, birds-eye maple, and white oak), walnut box (patterned inlay of mixed hardwoods), and walnut box (spalted maple lid).

BONUS TECHNIQUE

MIXING & MATCHING WOODS

Guidelines for adding punch to your next project

By Doug Stowe

When I began woodworking, I visited a lumberyard specializing in native Arkansas woods and was hooked. The varieties of grain and color both surprised and delighted me. Even the smell of each species caught my attention. As I returned to my shop I felt like I was on a mission to share my discovery of the beauty of our native woods. And so, after years of mixing and matching native woods, I've devised strategies for combining them effectively.

Beauty lies in the eye of the beholder, and not all craftsmen like the same combinations of woods. That's a good thing, as it allows each of us to find our own voice in our work. That said, it's easy to get carried away. Large projects can appear overly busy and distracting when too many colors (or woods) are put into play. Two seems comfortable; three, proceed with caution. On small boxes you can safely use more combinations so they stand out and get noticed.

To improve your awareness of how woods work together, consider these guidelines for a successful match.

Guidelines for success

Playing with contrasts in color and line, even texture, can serve as tools for calling attention to a craftsman's work. From the visual standpoint, they should tie in nicely with a project's final look and make good woodworking sense overall.

Contrasting colors and continuous grain can direct the eye. The sassafras and cherry in the left box are similar in value yet differ in tone. The miter keys and lighter wood color streaks of the box at right tie in with the lid.

The inside of this cherry box shows the difference between the original light color of the wood and the outside exposed surfaces.

Color

MANY WOODWORKERS FIND COLOR PERPLEXING, but unlike painters, we deal with a much simpler palette, making it harder to wander off course. Colors differ from each other in two ways, tone (red vs. green) and value or intensity (light to dark). A single piece of wood contains a collection of related colors within the wood grain. When matching woods, look for similarities in tone to provide a natural relationship as shown in the two boxes above. These often small similarities are your personal invitation to mix contrasting woods with confidence. The guideline: use woods that share a color relationship, be it ever so subtle.

Also, note that the color you see when you first cut a piece of wood may not be the final color. The effects of oxidation and sunlight are inevitable, especially on native species such as the cherry shown top right. The more you're aware of these effects, both in native and exotic woods, the more you can work them into your project's design.

Line

THE CONCEPT OF "LINE" IS MORE COMPLEX. While it can include the outline of the piece and the lines delineating the boundaries of parts, it has more to do with the lines of wood grain. Line leads the eye in exploring the finished work, like the sassafras and cherry box above. Matched door panels and edge-joined boards that show continuous lines or matching grain point to a woodworker's understanding (below). In addition to ensuring complementary edge-to-edge grain patterns, try to cut box sides from the same board

◀ How well grain lines interact reflects craftsmanship. These pieces of ash from a single board show from left to right a near match, and an obvious mismatch.

◀ Tight-grained walnut corner dowels and handcrafted hinges present a pleasing contrast with the pronounced flatsawn grain of this red oak box.

use these grains exclusively as shown in the Arts and Crafts coffee table, bottom left. In short, try to carefully mix and blend various grain patterns so they complement each other.

Texture

A THIRD CONTRASTING ELEMENT, TEXTURE, DEPARTS FROM A WOODWORKER'S OBSESSION WITH OBTAINING PERFECTLY SANDED SURFACES and is often overlooked. I frequently use both rough and finely finished surfaces in a box or piece of furniture, as the effects of weathering on wood, tool markings from its original milling, or a natural edge or defect provide character. The use of contrasting textures offers an invitation to the viewer to touch the work and explore with both hand and eye as with the two boxes above right.

and use them in sequence so the grain at mitered corners continues seamlessly. When mixing different species, however, divergent grain lines are expected in that they are separate pieces of wood and prove useful in accentuating contrast.

Some woods, such as maple and holly, have very fine, indistinct grain lines. In woods such as flatsawn oak, the grain is more pronounced. Fine or close grained woods better lend themselves to effective mixing than woods with more pronounced grain. This is especially true in frames where

the pronounced coarse grain of rails and stiles conflicts at joints. When choosing stock for pulls, accents, or handcrafted hinges, choose close-grained woods as in the box above left.

Woods that have a more pronounced grain require a greater level of attention. For example, when working with oak, familiarize yourself with how the wood is milled as shown below. Be warned that if you assemble a lot of flatsawn (or cathedral) grain parts throughout a project, they could fight with each other. If possible, mix in riftsawn and quartersawn stock or

This Arts and Crafts end table displays an attractive combination of quartersawn and riftsawn stock.

Quartersawn

Riftsawn

Flatsawn

This white oak box, with its weathered roughsawn red oak top panel, is made with contrasting walnut miter keys and pull. Contrasting textures beckon you to touch the piece while adding visual interest.

▼

▲

A walnut dovetailed box serves as the base to present the unique waney-edged spalted maple top. The placement of the hinges directs the eye to the natural edge overhanging the box and invites the hand to open it up.

Breaking the rules

AS WOODWORKERS, WE OFTEN END UP WITH EYE-CATCHING PIECES OF WOOD. Perhaps they're too small to make a whole box. Yet, we find these scraps so special that they deserve to be seen! I frequently use such woods as a contrasting panel in the top of a box, or, if suitable, as the entire lid. In a way, we're breaking the rules with such alluring pieces. Rather than blend in, such pieces play starring roles. A box lid panel can appear like art in a frame. When I choose the adjacent materials I think about woods that contrast the colors and grain of the starring piece. A wood with less distinct grain makes the best frame or base, allowing the starring piece to serve as the focal point (below). 🪵

Strategies for wood movement

WHENEVER YOU MIX WOODS, know that various species expand and contract at different rates, mostly across the grain. Simply gluing one species to another in a large piece of furniture can lead to joint failure. On small and large projects where you have frame-and-panel construction, whether of the same or different species, avoid joint failure by allowing the panel to "float" within the frame, as shown above left. For cutting boards and tabletops, consider capping end grain with breadboard ends. Minimize movement in parts by taking care to seal the ends and faces of all joint members.

This split walnut top with its rustic natural edge stands out against the plainer maple base.

▲

Raised-panel construction lets you frame a figured or otherwise special piece of wood, such as this quilted maple box top. By slightly undersizing the panel and letting it float (without glue) in the frame, you sidestep problems associated with expansion and contraction.

CRAFTSMAN'S TOOLBOX

Store chisels, marking tools, or whatever you like in this portable organizer

By Tim Birkeland and Jim Harrold

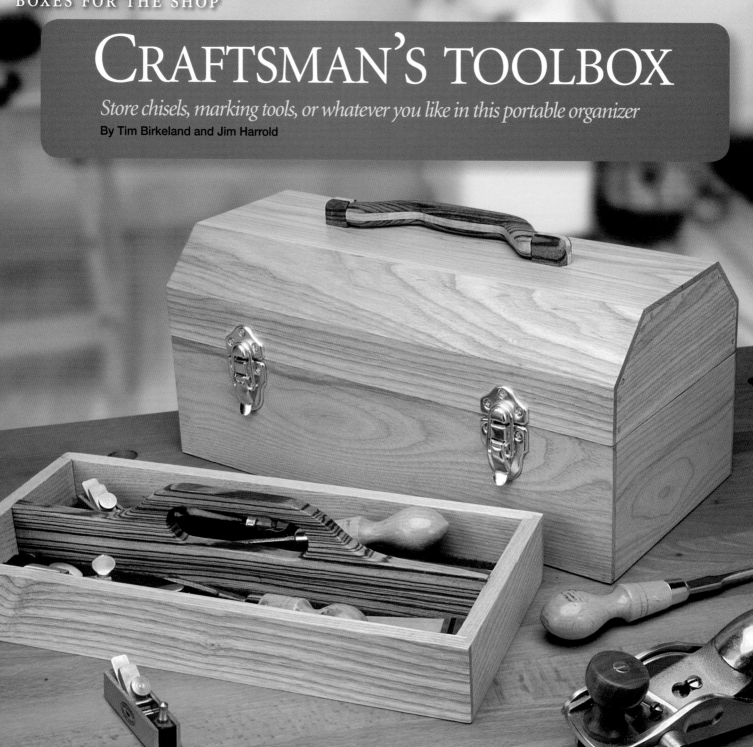

Overall dimensions: 16"w × 7⅞"d × 7¼"h

Toolboxes take a world of abuse over the years. Corners encounter dings, sides get scratched, and joints bust apart if the box falls hard on an unforgiving concrete floor. That's why the choices of wood and joint type are critical. For this practical design, we went with ash for its toughness and secured the box, lid, and lift-out tray with dovetail corner rabbets shown in the **Dovetail Rabbet Joint Detail** in **Figure 1**. The mechanical advantage of this joint over a standard rabbet joint is that dovetail parts grip each other, creating a more powerful bond. If you like, you can further enhance the joint—as we did— with ⅛"epoxied brass pins.

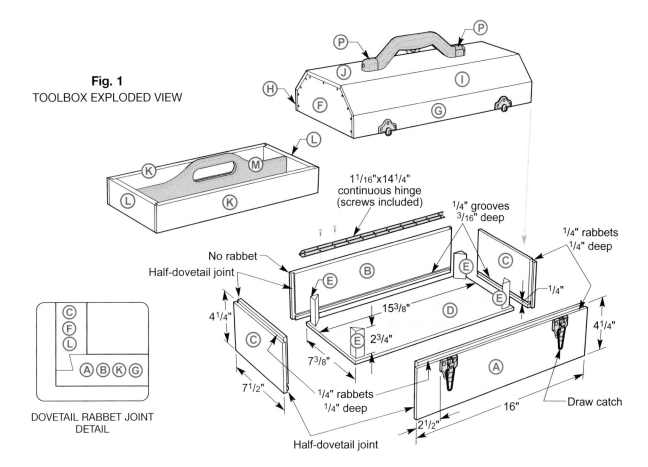

Fig. 1
TOOLBOX EXPLODED VIEW

1¹/₁₆"x14¹/₄" continuous hinge (screws included)

¹/₄" grooves ³/₁₆" deep

¹/₄" rabbets ¹/₄" deep

No rabbet

Half-dovetail joint

4¹/₄"

15³/₈"

¹/₄"

4¹/₄"

2³/₄"

7³/₈"

7¹/₂"

¹/₄" rabbets ¹/₄" deep

Half-dovetail joint

16"

2¹/₂"

Draw catch

DOVETAIL RABBET JOINT DETAIL

Begin with a nicely sized box

1 PLANE ENOUGH STOCK TO ½" THICK for the box sides (A) and (B), box ends (C), lid parts (F), (G), (H), (I), (J), and tray parts (K) and (L). See the **Cutting Diagram** and **Cut List** (page 93). Set aside a 12" long piece of ¾" stock for the tray supports (E).

2 USING PART OF THE PLANED STOCK, joint one edge and rip it to 4¼" wide. Now crosscut two sides to 16" long and two ends to 7½" long. (Machine extra pieces to the dimensions of the sides and ends for tool setups.) Finally, rip back side (B) to the finished width of 4".

3 CHUCK A 14° DOVETAIL BIT IN YOUR ROUTER TABLE and raise it just over one-half of the stock thickness of sides (A) and (B) and ends (C). Position the edge of the fence over the center of the bit. For testing, cut one half-dovetail end with the face of the extra end piece held to the fence as shown in **Photo A**. Cut the mating half dovetail with the side piece face down on the table as shown in **Photo B**. Test-fit the pieces together, and adjust the bit depth and fence until the joint is flush. See the **Dovetail Rabbet Joint Detail** in **Figure 1**. Now rout the ends of sides (A) and (B) and ends (C).

TIP ALERT
Label and keep test-cut mating ends of the locking dovetail joint for fast set-up later or future projects.

4 WITH A DADO SET IN YOUR TABLESAW, cut a ¼" rabbet ³/₁₆" deep. Adjust the fence ¼" from the cutter, and low enough to clear the half dovetail on the sides (A) and (B) and ends (C). Now cut the grooves for the box bottom where shown in **Figure 1**.

5 ADD A SACRIFICIAL FENCE to your tablesaw's fence and switch to a ⅜" dado set. Slide your sacrificial fence partially over the lowered dado set, lock it in place, and then turn on the saw, raising the dado set into the fence to ¼" high. Now adjust the fence to cut a ¼" rabbet ¼" deep along the top outside faces of the front side (A) and the ends (C). Make the cut as shown in **Photo C**.

Adjust the dovetail bit height and fence for a snug-fitting joint, using test pieces. Employ backer boards to prevent tear-out. Keep the test pieces handy for later setups.

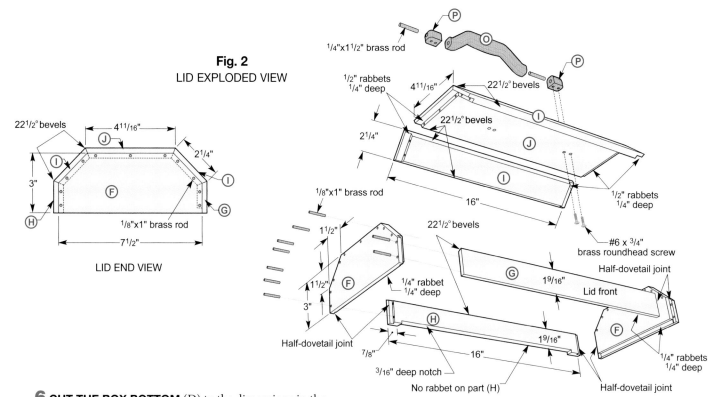

Fig. 2
LID EXPLODED VIEW

22½° bevels

4¹¹/₁₆"

J

2¼"

I

I

3"

F

H

1/8"x1" brass rod

G

7½"

LID END VIEW

¼"x1½" brass rod

P

O

P

½" rabbets ¼" deep

4¹¹/₁₆"

22½° bevels

22½° bevels

2¼"

I

J

I

16"

½" rabbets ¼" deep

1/8"x1" brass rod

1½"

1½"

3"

F

22½° bevels

G

1⁹/₁₆"

Lid front

Half-dovetail joint

#6 x ³/₄" brass roundhead screw

¼" rabbet ¼" deep

Half-dovetail joint

7/8"

H

1⁹/₁₆"

F

16"

³/₁₆" deep notch

No rabbet on part (H)

¼" rabbets ¼" deep

Half-dovetail joint

6 CUT THE BOX BOTTOM (D) to the dimensions in the **Cut List**. Test-fit the box assembly with the bottom in the grooves. If the joints remain tight all around, apply glue to the corners and permanently assemble the box as shown in **Photo D**. Otherwise, trim the bottom (D) to fit.

7 FINALLY, RETRIEVE THE 12" LENGTH OF ¾" STOCK, joint one edge, and bevel-rip the opposite edge at 45°. Adjust the blade to 90°, move the fence ¾" from the blade, and rip a beveled strip from the stock. Crosscut four 2¾" long pieces from the strip for tray supports (E). Glue one support in each inside corner of the box where shown in **Figure 1**, using spring clamps.

Now for the five-sided lid

1 FROM ½" STOCK, CUT TWO PIECES to 3 × 7½" and adhere them together with double-faced tape. Using either a mitersaw or tablesaw and miter gauge set at a 45° angle, angle-cut the top corners of the blanks 1½" up from the bottom edge to make the lid ends (F). Use a stopblock to guarantee identical cuts at each end.

2 SEPARATE THE LID ENDS (F) and cut a ¼" rabbet ¼" deep along their bottom edges where shown in **Figure 2**.

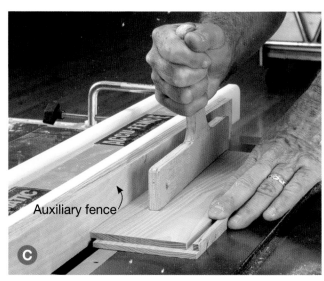

Auxiliary fence

C

Using an auxiliary fence attached to the tablesaw fence, cut the rabbets on the outside faces of the box front side and ends.

D

GLUE AND CLAMP the box sides, ends, and bottom as shown, checking for square.

3 **CUT THE FRONT VERTICAL STAVE** (G), back vertical stave (H), angled staves (I), and the top stave (J) to the lengths in the **Cut List** and ¼" wider to allow you to sneak up on beveled edges when fitting the pieces in place.

4 **MARK THE INSIDE FACES OF OPPOSING PARTS** and rout mating half-dovetail ends on the lid ends (F) and the ends of vertical staves (G) and (H) where shown in **Figure 2**, using the 14° dovetail bit and setup as before.

5 **WITH A DADO SET IN YOUR TABLESAW**, cut a ¼" rabbet ¼" deep along the inside bottom edge of front vertical stave (G). Now, switch to a wider dado set, and cut ½" rabbets ¼" deep on the inside ends of angled staves (I) and top stave (J). Note: Adjust the bit cut depth to achieve an end-grain seam that's identical with that of the box.

6 **REPLACE THE DADO SET** with a fine-tooth combination blade and angle it at 22½°. Next, with the piece face down, carefully bevel-rip the top edges of the vertical staves (G and H), holding the parts to the angle-cut ends (F) to check the fit. The heels of the bevels should intersect the end angles exactly. Temporarily tape the parts to the ends.

7 **BEVEL-RIP BOTH EDGES OF THE ANGLED STAVES** (I) at 22½°. Sneak up on the cuts until the heels of the bevels perfectly intersect with the angled cuts on the angle-cut ends (F). Test-fit the parts and tape them in place when satisfied. Finally, bevel-rip both edges of the top stave (J) and fit it in place where shown in **Figure 2**.

8 **GLUE-ASSEMBLE THE VERTICAL STAVES** (G, H) to the angle-cut ends (F) and let the half dovetails interlock. Check for square and let dry. Glue and fit the angled staves (I) in place, then,

Apply glue in the rabbets and on the beveled edges and fit the lid parts tightly together using blue painter's tape.

while the glue remains wet, glue and fit the centered top stave (J) in place. Secure these parts to the assembly with blue painter's tape as shown in **Photo E** to form the lid. Later, remove the tape and use a chisel to remove excess glue before it completely hardens. After the glue dries, sand the assembly to 220 grit.

Construct a handy tray

1 **CUT THE TRAY SIDES (K) AND ENDS (L)** from ash, and the divider/handle (M) from a contrasting wood (we used zebrawood) to the dimensions in the **Cut List**. Plane to ½" thick. Set the divider/handle (M) aside for now.

2 **USING THE ROUTER-TABLE SETUP** for the box and lid, cut the half dovetails for the ends of the tray sides (K) and ends (L) and test the fit of the dovetail joints at all four corners. Adjust if needed.

3 **CUT ¼" GROOVES** ³⁄₁₆" deep along the inside faces of the tray sides (K) and ends (L) for the bottom (N) where shown in **Figure 3**.

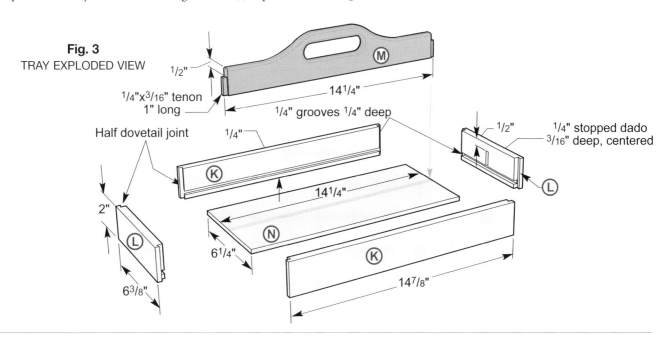

Fig. 3
TRAY EXPLODED VIEW
½"
¼"x³⁄₁₆" tenon 1" long
14¼"
¼" grooves ¼" deep
½"
¼" stopped dado ³⁄₁₆" deep, centered
Half dovetail joint
¼"
14¼"
2"
6¼"
6³⁄₈"
14⁷⁄₈"

4 MARK AND CUT out the centered ¼" wide, ³⁄₁₆" deep stopped dadoes on the ends (L) with a pair of sharp chisels as shown in **Photo F**.

5 MAKE A COPY of the **Tray Divider/ Handle Full-sized Half Pattern** on page 94. Trace it onto a ½" thick blank of contrasting wood. Flop it over at the centerline and trace again for a "whole" pattern.

6 BANDSAW THE OUTSIDE TOP EDGE of the divider/handle (M) to shape, staying just outside the cut line. Sand to the line (we used an oscillating spindle sander), and ease the edges.

7 DRILL THE TWO 1" DIAMETER HOLES in the handle opening on the pattern using a Forstner bit. Scrollsaw out the waste between the holes and sand the opening smooth, easing the edges.

8 CUT THE TENONS on the ends of the divider/handle (M) to shape on a tablesaw or router table, referring to the pattern on page 94.

9 CUT THE BOTTOM to the dimensions in the **Cut List** and dry-fit the tray pieces together. Now, glue-assemble the tray as shown in **Photo G** and clamp.

Add the handle and hardware

1 PLANE ENOUGH HARDWOOD STOCK to ¼" thick for an eye-catching handle. You'll need one 2 × 9" piece of ash, and two 2 × 9" pieces of a contrasting wood (we used zebrawood). Now, align and laminate the pieces to form the handle blank.

Use a mallet and 1" chisel to define the shoulders of the ³⁄₁₆" deep dadoes; go with a ¼" chisel to establish the end of the stopped dadoes and to clean out the waste.

Brush glue on all of the joints and clamp the tray parts together, checking for square. Later, remove squeeze-out, and sand the tray smooth, easing the edges.

2 SPRAY-ADHERE the **Toolbox Handle Full-sized Pattern** from page 94 to one face of the blank.

3 USING THE PATTERN AS A GUIDE, drill ¼" holes 1½" deep in the ends of the blank where indicated by **Step 1** on the pattern and as shown in **Photo H**.

4 FOLLOWING THE REMAINING FIVE STEPS in the pattern and **Photos I and J**, complete forming the laminated handle (O) and handle holders (P).

5 HAND-SAND OR MACHINE-SAND the bottom-most edges of the handle (O) where shown to allow it to rotate freely when secured to the lid. Test-fit with the ¼" brass pins in place. See **Step 5** on the pattern.

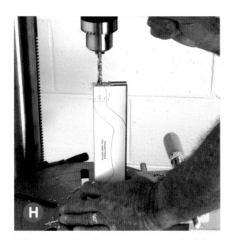

We used a hand screw clamp to hold the blank upright while drilling in the ends.

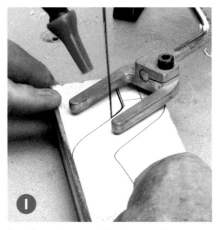

Scrollsaw just outside the cut line on the handle blank's pattern, then sand to the line.

Rout ¼" edges on the handle (O) and top and end edges of the handle holders (P). Don't rout the lower edge of the holders.

TIP ALERT Maintain safe control when routing small parts like the toolbox handle by using a pushpad to keep fingers out of harm's way.

6 CUT TWO ¼" BRASS PINS to 1½" long and epoxy them into the holes in the handle holders (P), leaving the outside pin ends proud. After the epoxy cures, sand or file the outside edges of the pins flush with the outside edges of the handle holders (P). Next, fit the protruding ends of the pins into the holes at each end of the handle (O). Now, center, glue, and screw the handle (O) and handle holders (P) assembly to the lid where shown in **Figure 2** using #6 × ¾ brass round head screws.

7 CUT A 14¼" LENGTH of 1¹⁄₁₆" wide continuous (piano) brass hinge. Using the hinge length as a guide, center and mark the location of the hinge on the bottom edge of the back vertical stave (H). Now, set up your router table with a ⅜" straight bit raised ⅝" and set the fence ³⁄₁₆" from the front edge of the bit. Set up the fence stops and, with the lid on edge (part H face down), cut the stopped notch where shown in **Figure 4**. Square the corners of the notch with a sharp chisel.

Fig. 4
NOTCH DETAIL

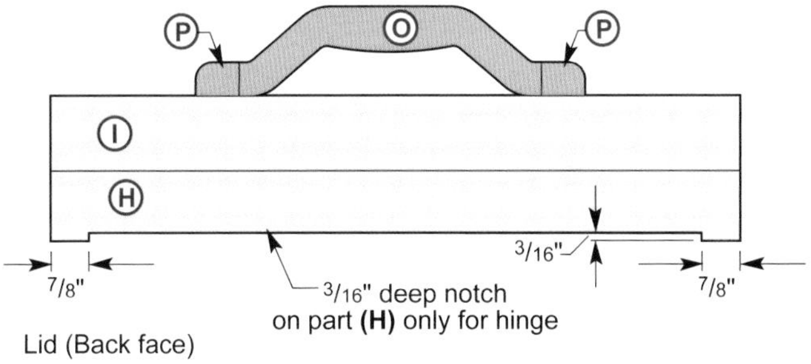

P
O
P
I
H
7/8"
3/16"
3/16" deep notch on part (H) only for hinge
7/8"

Lid (Back face)

8 TEMPORARILY INSTALL THE HINGE to the box and lid. Test the fit and adjust if needed. Temporarily add the latch hardware. Remove the hinge and latches and finish-sand the toolbox to 220 grit.

9 OPTIONAL: DRILL 22 HOLES into the ends of the box and lid where shown in **Figure 2**. Now, cut 22 pins 1" long from a ⅛" diameter brass rod and epoxy them in place, sanding them flush. Doing this adds both an aesthetic touch and strength.

10 FINISH THE BOX. (We used Arm-R-Seal Oil and Urethane Topcoat.) Now reattach the hardware.

11 OPTIONAL: LINE THE BOX and tray bottoms with adhesive-backed felt to protect prized tools and add class to a well-made project.

Convenience-PLUS BUYING GUIDE	
	ITEM
☐ 1.	**Whiteside 14° Dovetail Bit, ½" D, ½" C, (½" SH)**
☐ 2.	**Woodcraft Anti-kickback Roundover Bit, ¼" R, ½" CL (¼" SH)**
☐ 3.	**Premium Brass Piano Hinge, 1¹⁄₁₆"×4'**
☐ 4.	**General Finishes Arm-R-Seal Oil & Urethane Topcoat, Satin, Pint**
☐ 5.	**Cloth-backed, Pressure Sensitive Adhesive Felt Sheet, 35¾"×23", Green**
☐ 6.	**Draw Catch, Brass, 2¾"×1½"**
☐ 7.	**Available at hardware stores and hobby shops: ⅛" Brass Rod and ¼" Brass Rod**

Cutting Diagram

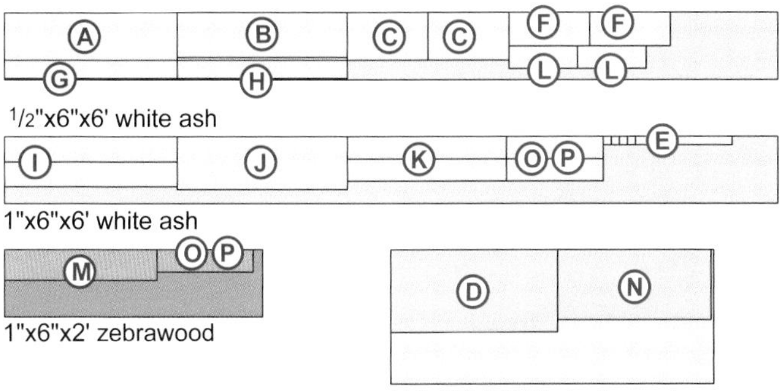

A
B
C
C
F
F
G
H
L
L
1/2"x6"x6' white ash
I
J
K
O
P
E
1"x6"x6' white ash
M
O
P
1"x6"x2' zebrawood
D
N
1/4"x12"x30" birch plywood

Craftsman's Toolbox Cut List		Thickness	Width	Length	Qty.	Mat'l
Box						
A	Front side	½"	4¼"	16"	1	WA
B	Back side	½"	4"	16"	1	
C	Ends	½"	4¼"	7½"	2	WA
D	Bottom	¼"	7⅜"	15⅜"	1	BP
E	Shelf supports	¾"	¾"	2¾"	4	WA
Lid						
F	Angle-cut ends	½"	3"	7½"	2	WA
G*	Front vertical stave	½"	1⁹⁄₁₆"	16"	1	WA
H*	Back vertical stave	½"	1⁹⁄₁₆"	16"	1	WA
I*	Angled staves	½"	2¼"	16"	2	WA
J*	Top stave	½"	4¹¹⁄₁₆"	16"	1	WA
Tray						
K	Sides	½"	2"	14⅞"	2	WA
L	Ends	½"	2"	6⅜"	2	WA
M	Divider/handle	½"	2¾"	14¼"	1	ZW
N	Bottom	¼"	6¼"	14¼"	1	BP
Handle						
O	Laminated handle	¾"	2"	7"	1	ZW/WA
P	Laminated holders	¾"	¾"	1	2	ZW/WA

*Variances in width of beveled parts require you to cut them slightly wider and sneak up on the finished width, test-fitting to the ends and mating parts as you go.
WA=White Ash ZW=Zebrawood BP=Birch Plywood

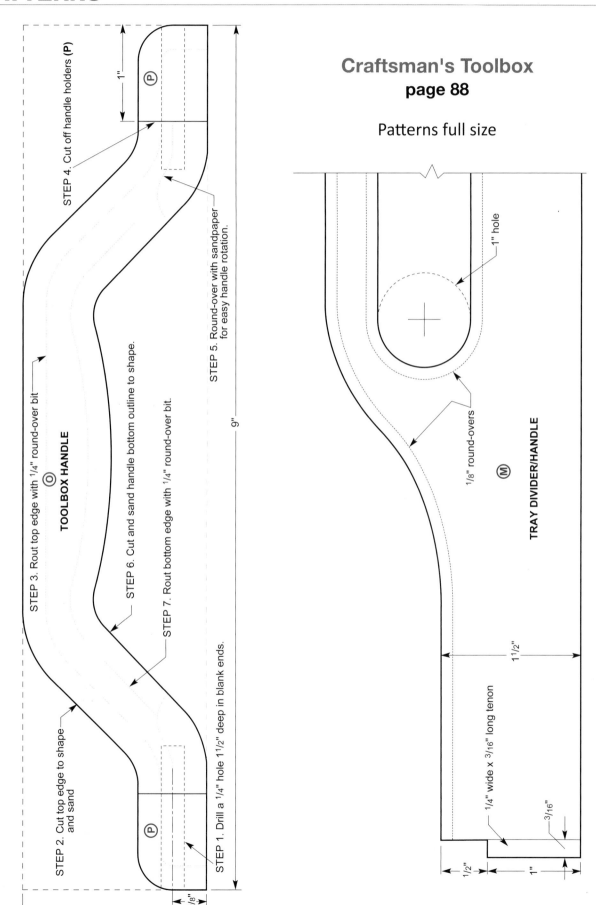

Craftsman's Toolbox
page 88

Patterns full size

TOOLBOX HANDLE

STEP 1. Drill a 1/4" hole 1 1/2" deep in blank ends.

STEP 2. Cut top edge to shape and sand

STEP 3. Rout top edge with 1/4" round-over bit

STEP 4. Cut off handle holders (P)

STEP 5. Round-over with sandpaper for easy handle rotation.

STEP 6. Cut and sand handle bottom outline to shape.

STEP 7. Rout bottom edge with 1/4" round-over bit.

1"

9"

2"

3/8"

(P)

TRAY DIVIDER/HANDLE

1" hole

1/8" round-overs

1 1/2"

1/4" wide x 3/16" long tenon

3/16"

1/2"

1"

(M)

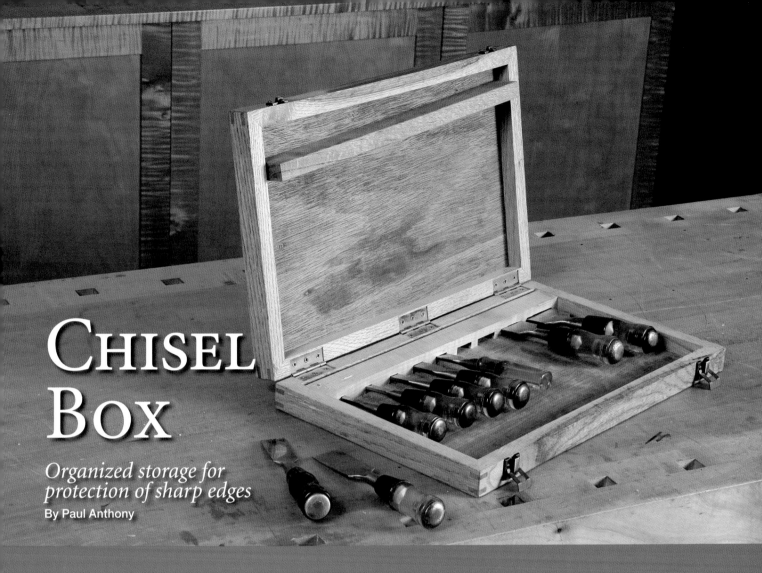

CHISEL BOX

Organized storage for
protection of sharp edges

By Paul Anthony

When it comes to hand tool storage, chisels present a special challenge. Their sharp edges can inflict damage as well as suffer it, so if your chisels are rattling around in a drawer, or still in flimsy original packaging, consider making a box to protect and organize them for easy retrieval. I based this design on a very old version that I once saw for carving tools. It's simple, ingenious, and can be sized to suit any chisel set. The chisels slip neatly into dadoes in a separator block while a retaining strip attached to the box top keeps them in place when carrying the closed box around the shop or to a job site. The box requires just a few lengths of ¾" thick solid wood for the walls and some ¼" hardwood plywood for the top and bottom. Construction is simple, because you assemble the box as a closed unit and then rip through its center to create the top and bottom.

Sizing the box

To determine the front-to-back interior length (IL) of the box, measure the length of your longest chisel and add 1¼". Next, lay out your chisels side by side in ascending length, with the bevels facing downward. (Work on a surface where you can leave the layout undisturbed while making the box.) Space them apart about ½". Measure the span of the set, and then add 1" to determine the box's interior width (IW). To calculate the interior height (IH), lay a strip of wood atop the chisel butts and add ⅛" to that height. Now you can determine the finished lengths and widths of your box sides using the equations in **Figure 1**.

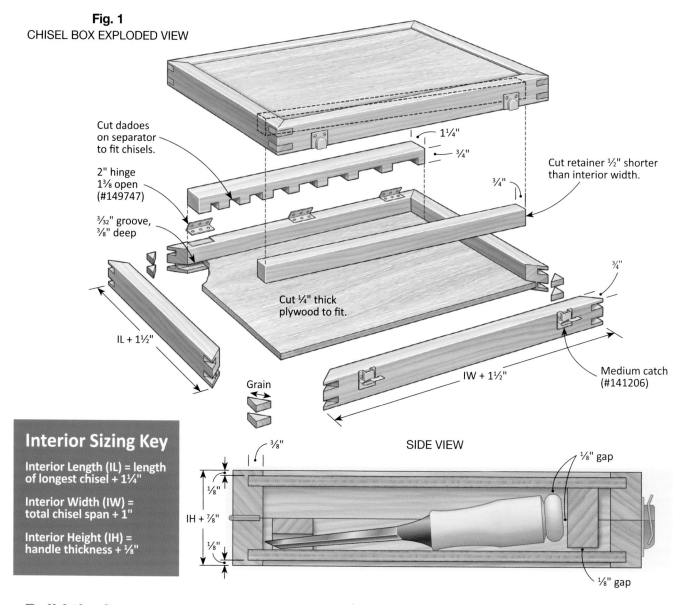

Fig. 1
CHISEL BOX EXPLODED VIEW

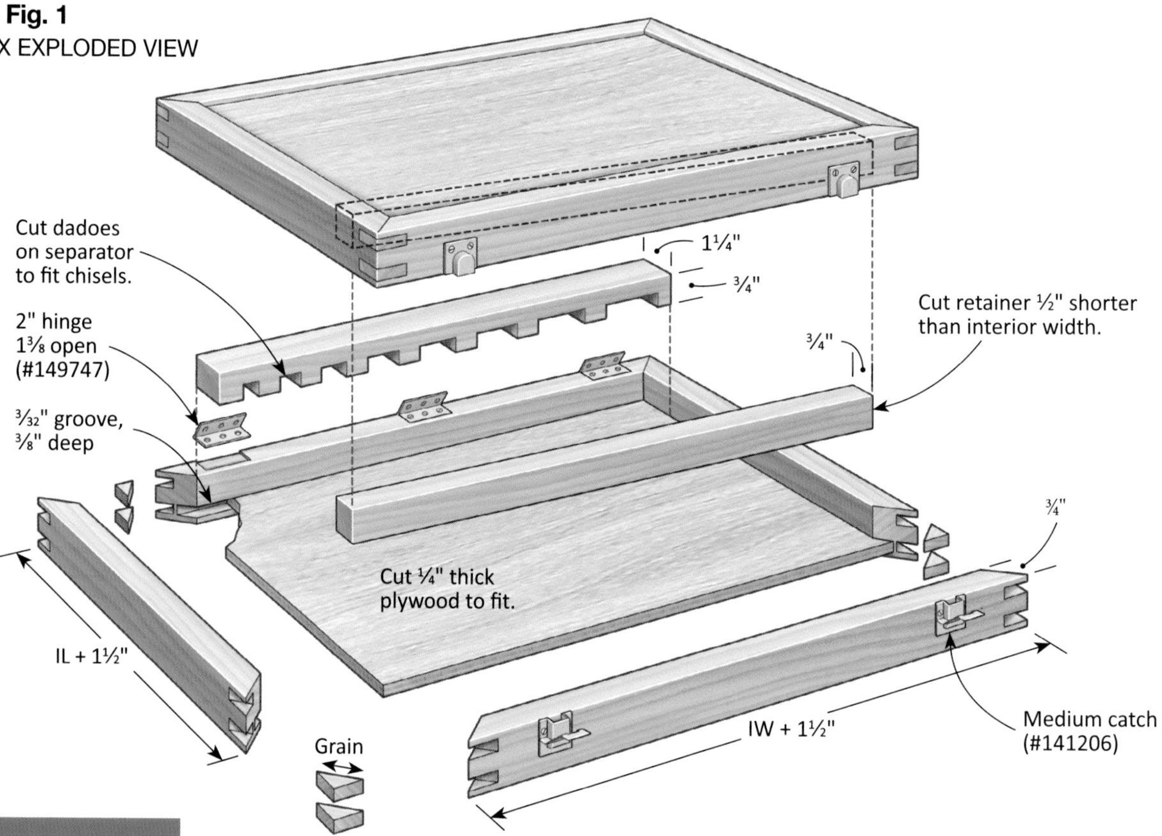

Cut dadoes on separator to fit chisels.
2" hinge 1 3/8 open (#149747)
3/32" groove, 3/8" deep
IL + 1 1/2"
1 1/4"
3/4"
3/4"
Cut retainer 1/2" shorter than interior width.
3/4"
Cut 1/4" thick plywood to fit.
Grain
IW + 1 1/2"
Medium catch (#141206)

Interior Sizing Key

Interior Length (IL) = length of longest chisel + 1 1/4"

Interior Width (IW) = total chisel span + 1"

Interior Height (IH) = handle thickness + 1/8"

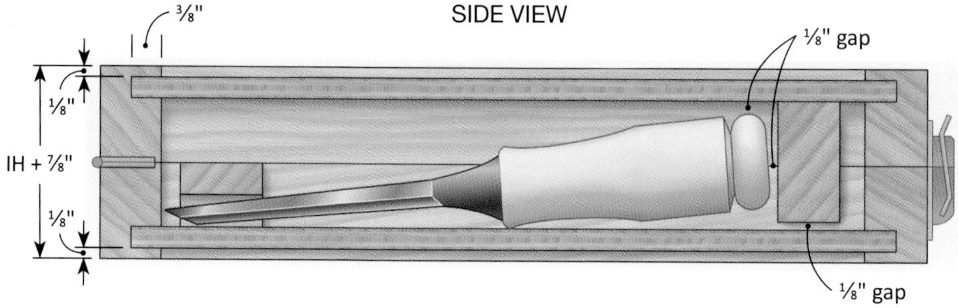

SIDE VIEW
3/8"
1/8"
IH + 7/8"
1/8"
1/8" gap
1/8" gap

Build the box

1 CUT THE SIDES TO SIZE from 3/4" thick hardwood and miter both ends of each. Saw the 3/8" deep panel grooves 1/8" in from each edge, making them just wide enough to snugly accept 1/4" thick hardwood plywood (which is actually about 3/32" thick).

2 DRY-CLAMP THE SIDES TOGETHER with a band clamp, measure for the panels, and cut the two plywood pieces to size. Apply glue to the grooves and mitered ends, insert the panels, and then clamp the box together. Make sure the assembly is flat and square under clamp pressure.

3 LAY OUT AND SAW FOUR SPLINE SLOTS in each corner, accounting for the kerf you'll make when sawing the sides apart. Glue splines in the slots. When the glue dries, trim them flush.

4 ADJUST YOUR TABLESAW BLADE HEIGHT to 7/8", and set the fence to slice the sides down their center. Cut through three sides, and then clamp shims into the kerfs before making the final cut. The shims will keep the separated sides from collapsing onto the blade at the end of the cut.

5 MAKE THE SEPARATOR from a piece of 3/4" × 1 1/4" hardwood, crosscutting it to fit between the box sides. Then take the separator over to your organized chisels, place its edge against the chisel tips, and transfer their blade widths to the edge of the separator. Cut the dadoes, test the chisels for fit, and glue the separator to the box bottom. (You can slide the separator closer to the chisel handles to close up gaps above the chisel blades.)

6 MORTISE THE BOX BOTTOM AND TOP for two or three hinges and install them. Also, install the catches.

7 FINALLY, MAKE THE RETAINER from 3/4" thick stock, crosscutting it about 1/2" shorter than the interior box width. Rip it to a width equal to the box interior height, and apply double-faced tape to one edge. Place it tape side up in the box bottom about 1/8" from the chisel butts, and press the lid against it. Open the lid, trace around the retainer, remove it, and rip 1/8" from one edge. Glue and clamp it in place within your traced lines. Done.

Overall dimensions:
21"w × 11¼"d × 13¼" h

SANDPAPER
STORAGE BOX

Organize sheets, discs, pads, and more in this tamboured tote box.

By Chuck Hedlund

W ho doesn't need flexible, dedicated storage to keep sandpaper and sanding accessories sorted and easy to access? This plywood box provides multiple slide-out trays in two sizes for a variety of needs. You can even further divide the trays with divider strips if you so desire. To shut

out dust, I designed a pull-down tambour door that you make or buy, depending on your budget. And to tote the box around the shop, reach for the finger-friendly handles drilled through the sides. Another plus is the corralled top that can serve as a cutting station for sizing sheets for your pad sander and sanding blocks.

Note: Because plywood thicknesses come slightly under the dimensions in the plan, measure your plywood and make any needed adjustments when machining the dadoes and rabbets.

*See the **Convenience-Plus Buying Guide** on page 101 for a list of materials and supplies used to make this project.*

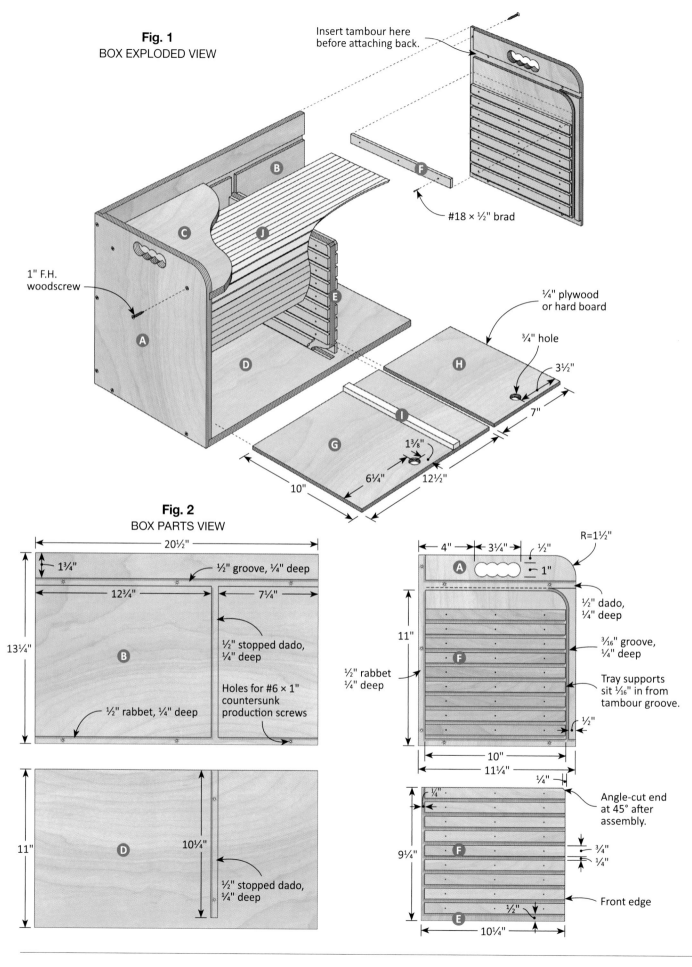

Fig. 1
BOX EXPLODED VIEW

Insert tambour here
before attaching back.

#18 × ½" brad

1" F.H.
woodscrew

¼" plywood
or hard board

¾" hole

3½"

7"

10"

6¼"

12½"

1⅜"

Fig. 2
BOX PARTS VIEW

20½"

1¾"

½" groove, ¼" deep

12¾"

7¼"

13¼"

½" stopped dado,
¼" deep

Holes for #6 × 1"
countersunk
production screws

½" rabbet, ¼" deep

11"

10¼"

½" stopped dado,
¼" deep

R=1½"

4"

3¼"

½"

1"

11"

½" dado,
¼" deep

³⁄₁₆" groove,
¼" deep

Tray supports
sit ¹⁄₁₆" in from
tambour groove.

½" rabbet
¼" deep

½"

10"

11¼"

¼"

¼"

Angle-cut end
at 45° after
assembly.

9¼"

¾"

¼"

Front edge

½"

10¼"

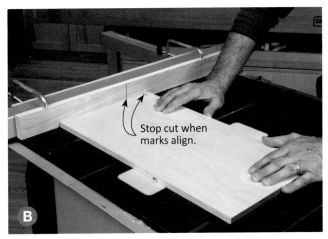

With the plywood bottom contacting the dado set, mark this leading edge on the fence as shown.

Ease the piece into the dado set, stopping when the marks align. Chisel the stopped dado square.

First, the box

1 CUT THE SIDES (A), back (B), top (C), bottom (D), and divider (E) to the sizes listed in the **Cut List**. Mark out the radii in the upper front corners in the sides in **Figure 1**. Also, note that the left and right sides mirror each other, as do the stopped dado locations in the top and bottom.

2 ATTACH A SACRIFICIAL FENCE to your tablesaw fence, and install a dado set and zero-clearance insert. Now, using the **Box Parts View** in **Figure 2**, lay out and cut the ¼" deep rabbets and full-length dadoes in the sides (A) and back (B).

3 LAY OUT THE STOPPED DADOES in the back (B) and bottom (D) for divider (E). Now set the fence at 12¾" from the dado set. Use the bottom to establish where the front end of the dado set contacts the workpiece, and mark the auxiliary fence **(Photo A)**. Make a second mark on the outside face of the workpiece and ¾" in from the trailing edge by the fence.

4 TURN ON THE SAW AND CUT the stopped dado in the bottom (D) as shown in **Photo B**. Turn off the saw when the mark on the bottom aligns with the one on the fence. Square the dado.

5 SET THE FENCE 7¼" from the inside teeth of the dado set, mark the outside face of back (B), and make the

stopped dado on the inside face. Square the stopped dado as before.

6 DRY-FIT THE BOX PARTS WITH CLAMPS. Next, mark and drill the countersunk pilot holes in sides (A), back (B), and bottom (D) where shown in **Figure 2**.

7 CUT A PIECE OF ¼" HARDBOARD or plywood to at least 12 × 12" for the template for routing the tambour door groove. Bandsaw and sand a 1½" radius on one corner.

8 AS SHOWN IN FIGURE 3, CLAMP THE TEMPLATE IN PLACE on the inside face of one side (A). Now, set up a handheld router with a 7/16" OD guide

bushing and a 3/16" straight bit adjusted to cut ½" deep (the thickness of the template plus ¼").

9 NEXT, ROUT THE TAMBOUR TRACK GROOVE in one side (A), using the bushing to guide against the template. Relocate the template onto the mirroring side, and rout the remaining tambour groove.

10 BANDSAW THE 1½" RADII on the front top corners of sides (A). Sand smooth.

11 MARK OUT THE HANDLE OPENINGS in the sides (A) using **Figure 2**. Now drill overlapping holes with a 1" Forstner bit.

Fig. 3
TEMPLATE ROUTING SETUP

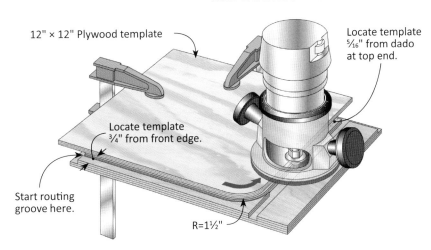

12" × 12" Plywood template

Locate template 5/16" from dado at top end.

Locate template ¾" from front edge.

Start routing groove here.

R=1½"

Make the trays and tray supports

1 CUT THE TRAY SUPPORTS (F) to size.

2 NOW PLACE THE DIVIDER (E) on a flat surface. Cut a ¼" thick spacer from scrap. Referring to **Figure 2,** start at the top edge of the divider and fasten the tray supports (F) flush with the front edge with glue and brads **(Photo C)**. Use the spacer to locate and fasten the supports to the divider's other side and inside faces of sides (A).

3 NEXT, ASSEMBLE THE BOX with glue and screws, but do not attach the back (B).

4 CUT THE LARGE TRAYS (G) and the small trays (H) to size. You will need about 1/32" clearance between the sides (A) and divider (E) for easy sliding.

5 WITH A ¾" FORSTNER BIT, bore the finger pulls on the large trays (G) and the small trays (H).

6 TO ORGANIZE NARROWER SANDPAPER strips for your block sanders, customize the trays by cutting, gluing, and nailing tray dividers (I) as shown in **Figure 1**.

7 WITH THE BACK (B) removed, apply two to three coats of protective finish (we used clear satin water-based polyurethane) to the box, sanding between each one.

Tape used for contrast.

After securing the first tray support along the top edge with glue and brads, use a spacer to fasten the remaining supports.

Tambour door options

OPTION 1: PREMADE TAMBOUR

1 WORKING FROM ONE END OF A COILED TAMBOUR ROLL, mark the needed door length. To determine the length, measure the door opening plus the groove depths, minus 1/16".

2 NOW, ELEVATE THE TAMBOUR ROLL FOR CLEARANCE, and cut it proud of the marked length **(Photo D)**. Unroll the workpiece, and, placing the factory edge against your tablesaw fence, cut it to finished length. Proceed to the next section for installation.

OPTION 2: SHOP MADE TAMBOUR

1 PLANE A 24" LENGTH OF STOCK to ½" thick. Now, adjust your saw fence and rip 22 tambour strips (J) to 5/32" thick using a sharp 40-tooth or greater saw blade with a zero-clearance throat plate and splitter for the smoothest cut.

Start with a jointed edge and rip the strip to thickness. Repeat the jointing and ripping until you have the needed number. Ensure the strips are straight and flat, cutting extras if needed. Now, mark the sawn sides to indicate the inside faces.

2 NEXT, CROSSCUT THE STRIPS (J) to 207/16" long using a stopblock.

3 PLACE A FRAMING SQUARE ON A FLAT SURFACE and clamp it down so it can't move. Lay the strips (J)—backsides facing up—so the first strip is against the long arm of the square and tight in the corner. Place the other strips alongside one another. Now snug them together and firmly secure the assembly with four evenly spaced lengths of Gorilla Tape **(Photo E)**. Space the outside tape lengths ¾" in from the ends of the strips. With a utility knife, cut

Use a fine-toothed handsaw to cut the premade tambour roll, supporting it as shown.

Start tape ¾" from end.

Secure the tambour strips with Gorilla Tape evenly spaced across the inside face.

F

Align the ends of the tambour door with the grooves, and slide the door in place, raising and lowering it to test the action.

Cutting and Sizing Sheets

To cut sheet sandpaper for sanding blocks and pad sanders, make cutting templates to the most-used sizes (½", ¼", and ⅓" sheet) from ⅛" acrylic. Slice the sheets with a rotary cutter on a cutting mat using the templates to speed your work. This approach allows you to better control the depth of cut while proving safer overall, and you can store all the items on top of the tote.

the tape where the square and the first strip meet. Next, cut the tape flush along the outside edge of the outside strip.

> **TIP ALERT**
> To ensure a tight edge-to-edge fit for the tambour strips, snug them with masking tape prior to applying the Gorilla Tape.

Finally, install the tambour door

1 DRILL A PILOT HOLE FOR THE KNOB attachment screw centered in the second strip (J) from the bottom edge of the assembled tambour door. Now, slide the door into the groove from the back of the box **(Photo F)** and check the fit.

2 WITH THE DOOR IN PLACE, insert a screw through the tambour and thread on the knob. Screw on the back, open the door, and slip in the trays. Add the sandpaper sheets and discs and other sanding accessories. 🪚

Convenience–PLUS BUYING GUIDE

	ITEM
☐ 1.	*Finnish Birch Plywood, ¼ × 24 × 30", qty. 4
☐ 2.	*Finnish Birch Plywood, ½ × 24 × 30", qty. 3
☐ 3.	Brass Bushing, ⁷⁄₁₆" OD × 1¹⁄₃₂" ID
☐ 4.	Straight Bit, ³⁄₁₆" D, ½" CL (¼" SH)
☐ 5.	Round-over Bit, ⅛" R (¼" SH)
☐ 6.	General Finishes Polyacrylic Water-based Topcoat, Satin, 1 pt.
☐ 7.	Pole Wrap, Maple, 10¾" × 8' $65-$75
☐ 8.	Gorilla Tape, 1⅞" wide × 36'

Sandpaper Storage Box Cut List

		Thickness	Width	Length	Qty.	Mat'l
A	Side	½"	11¼"	13¼"	2	FBP
B	Back	½"	13¼"	20½"	1	FBP
C	Top	½"	11"	20½"	1	FBP
D	Bottom	½"	11"	20½"	1	FBP
E	Divider	½"	10¼"	9¼	1	FBP
F	Tray supports	¼"	¾"	10"	36	FBP
G	Large tray	¼"	10"	12½"	9	FBP
H	Small tray	¼"	10"	7"	9	FBP
I	Tray dividers	⅜"	⅝"	10"	TBD	P
J*	Shop-made tambour	⁵⁄₃₂"	½"	20⁷⁄₁₆"	21	M

*Assembled shop-made tambour door should measure 11 × 20⁷⁄₁₆"; purchased tambour should measure 10¾ × 20⁷⁄₁₆". Both work in this application.
Materials: FBP=Finnish Birch Plywood, P=Pine, M=Maple
Supplies: (21) #6 × 1" flathead wood screws; #18 × ½" wire brads; for pull, ³⁄₁₆ × ¼" binding post with screw and #6 SAE washer; ⅛" acrylic; cutting mat; rotary cutter (fabric store).

FOLDING SHOP BOX

Fast storage when you need it.

By Scott Phillips and Jim Harrold

> *"Clutter is the thing that gets out of control in almost every shop. One of my favorite ways to manage tools is with this featured collapsible shop box. This 1920s design is the right way to put everything in its place. Plus they stack for even better storage. It's a keeper."*

When is a box not a box? When you can fold it up and store it flat in a wink. This hinge-happy carry-all consists of scrap plywood and common hardware. A workshop favorite of Scott Phillips, host of *The American Woodshop* on PBS, the shop box lets you tote tools and materials from place to place, store turning blanks, and contain valuable cut-offs. Construction couldn't be simpler. Let's build one.

Build the Basic Box

1 CUT TWO BOX SIDES (A) and two ends (B) (we used Baltic birch) to the sizes shown in the **Cut List** (page 103) from ½" thick scrap plywood. Then cut the bottom (C) from ¾" thick plywood.

2 RETURN TO THE ENDS (B) and mark two center points for the 6" handle openings where shown in the Box Exploded View, **Figure 1**. Drill the 1¼" holes, strike cut lines at the top and bottom of the holes to connect them, and then jigsaw or scrollsaw out the elongated openings to form the box handles. Rout ⅛" round-overs around the openings on both faces of

each end (B) to ease the sharp edges for carrying the box.

3 NEXT, CUT FOUR TRIANGULAR CORNER FEET (D) and two rectangular edge feet (E) from ¼" thick scrap plywood. See the dimensions in **Figure 1**. Glue and clamp these pieces onto the bottom face of the box bottom (C) where shown. (If you plan on finishing your box, do this now before assembly.)

TIP ALERT
The screws that come with the hardware are too long for ½" plywood. Instead of buying shorter screws, simply snip the tips so they don't poke through.

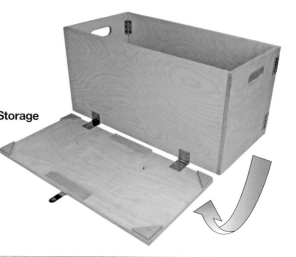

Collapsing the Box for Easy Storage
To fold up your shop box simply unhook the bottom, let the bottom drop down, and collapse the sides.

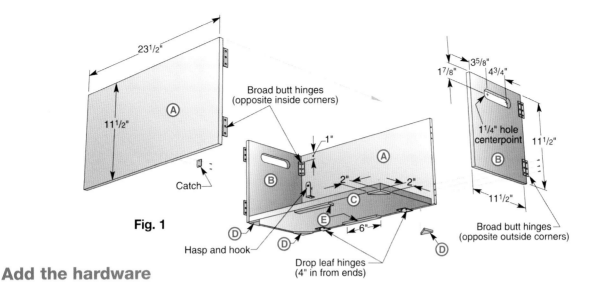

Broad butt hinges
(opposite inside corners)

23½"

11½"

Ⓐ

Catch

Fig. 1

Hasp and hook

Ⓐ

Ⓑ

Ⓒ

Ⓔ

Ⓓ

Ⓓ

1"

2"

2"

6"

Drop leaf hinges
(4" in from ends)

3⅝"

1⅞"

4¾"

1¼" hole
centerpoint

Ⓑ

11½"

11½"

Ⓓ

Broad butt hinges
(opposite outside corners)

Add the hardware

**1 STAND ONE SIDE (A) AND ONE END (B) ON THEIR
BOTTOM EDGES** and butt the side against the inside face
of the end, ensuring that the outside face of the side is flush
with the end's edge (see the hinge locations in **Figure 1**).
Place a broad butt hinge in the inside corner 1" down from
the top edge. Start the screw holes with an awl or Vix bit, and
then drive the screws. Place a second broad butt hinge 1" up
from the bottom inside corner and secure it. Apply a pair of
broad butt hinges to the remaining side and end, creating an
opposing second side/end assembly.

**2 CLAMP THE TWO SIDE/END ASSEMBLIES
TOGETHER,** with the ends butting against the inside face of
the sides. Mark the locations of the outside broad butt hinges
where shown and drive the screws in the outside face of ends
(B) and edges of the sides (A). You should now have an open-
ended box.

**3 FIT THE BOX BOTTOM IN THE HINGED BOX
ASSEMBLY** and attach the drop leaf hinges along one outside
face of one box side where shown. With the bottom face of
the box bottom (C) flush with the bottom edges of the box
assembly, fasten the remaining leaves to the box bottom.

4 CENTER AND INSTALL THE HASP WITH HOOK on the
top face of bottom (C) opposite the edge having the drop leaf
hinges. Raise the hasp leaf to determine the catch location
and install it. Using a sanding block and 150 grit, ease all
exposed sharp edges. Now check out the photo sequence to
see how to fold up the box for easy storage. 🪚

Convenience +PLUS BUYING GUIDE	
	ITEM
☐ 1.	**2 x 1⅜" Broad Butt Hinges (4 Pr)**
☐ 2.	**Drop Leaf Table Hinges (1 Pr)**
☐ 3.	**Solid Brass Hasp with Hook**

Folding Shop Box Cut List		Thickness	Width	Length	Qty.	Mat'l
A	Sides	½"	11½"	23½"	2	BP
B	Ends	½"	11½"	11½"	2	BP
C	Bottom	¾"	11"	23"	1	BP
D	Corner feet	¼"	2"	2"	4	BP
E	Edge feet	¼"	1"	6"	2	BP
F*	Frame for feet	½"	¾"	2×2"	4	W
G	Front and back	¼"	1 ⅛"	5 ½"	2	W
H	Notched sides	¼"	1 ⅛"	5 ½"	2	W
I	Bottom	¼"	5 ¼"	5 ¼"	1	FW

BP = Birch Plywood (or scrap fir plywood of the same thickness)

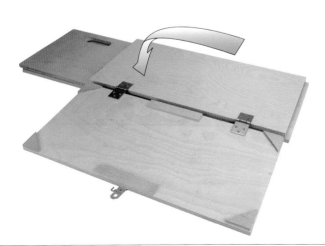

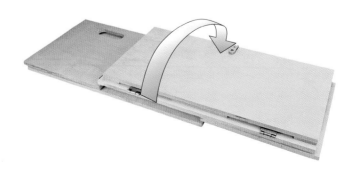

PROJECT CREDITS

GREAT GIFT BOXES	Designer	Builder	Writer	Photographer	Illustrator
6 Sweetheart's Music Box	Stephen Johnson	Stephen Johnson	Bob Settich	Ken Brady and Chad McClung	Roxanne LeMoine
14 Splined Keepsake Box	Paul Anthony	Paul Anthony	Paul Anthony	Doug Rowan and Paul Anthony	Roxanne LeMoine
20 Coved Jewelry Box	Geoff Noden	Geoff Noden	Paul Anthony	Paul Anthony	James Provost
25 Collector's Showcase	Craig Bentzley	Craig Bentzley	Craig Bentzley	Jim Osborn and Paul Anthony	Roxanne LeMoine
33 Bonus Technique: Lining Drawers with Fabric	Craig Bentzley	Craig Bentzley	Craig Bentzley	Jim Osborn and Paul Anthony	
36 Pagoda-style Jewelry Box	Bob Dickey	Bob Dickey	Bob Dickey	Doug Edmonds	Mario Ferro
46 Curved-Top Veneered Box	Jonathan Benson	Jonathan Benson	Jonathan Benson	Jim Osborn and Paul Anthony	John Hartman
52 Bonus Technique: No-Fear Veneering	Jonathan Benson	Jonathan Benson	Jonathan Benson	Paul Anthony	
BOXES FOR THE HOME	Designer	Builder	Writer	Photographer	Illustrator
59 Country-Loving Salt Box	Scott Phillips/ American Woodshop	Scott Phillips/ Valerie White (painted)	Scott Phillips	Ken Brady	Shane Wiersma
64 Steak Knives & Presentation Box	Andy Rae	Andy Rae	Andy Rae	Andy Rae	Roxanne LeMoine
NOVELTY BOXES	Designer	Builder	Writer	Photographer	Illustrator
71 Post Office Box Piggy Bank	A.J. Hamler	A.J. Hamler	A.J. Hamler	Jim Osborn	Shane Wiersma
77 Magic Coin Box	Ken Burton	Ken Burton	Ken Burton	Jim Osborn and Paul Anthony	Frank Rohrbach
84 Bonus Technique: Mixing & Matching Woods	Doug Stowe	Doug Stowe	Doug Stowe	Doug Stowe	
BOXES FOR THE SHOP	Designer	Builder	Writer	Photographer	Illustrator
88 Craftsman's Tool Box	Tim Birkeland	Tim Birkeland	Jim Harrold	Ken Brady and Chad McClung	Roxanne LeMoine
95 Chisel Box	Paul Anthony	Paul Anthony	Paul Anthony	Paul Anthony	Frank Rohrbach
97 Sandpaper Storage Box	Chuck Hedlund	Chuck Hedlund	Jim Harrold	Jim Osborn	Mario Ferro
102 Folding Shop Box	Scott Phillips/ American Woodshop	Tim Birkeland	Jim Harrold	Ken Brady	Roxanne LeMoine